the Idler book of

CRAP VACATIONS

50 TALES OF HELL ON EARTH

Compiled and Edited by Dan Kieran

Harper

An Imprint of HarperCollins*Publishers*

A hardcover edition of this book was published in Great Britain in 2005 by Bantam Books.

HarperCollins books may be purchased for educational, business, or sales promotional use. For information please write: Special Markets Department, HarperCollins Publishers, 10 East 53rd Street, New York, NY 10022.

First Harper paperback published 2006.

Library of Congress Cataloging-in-Publication Data
The Idler book of crap vacations : 50 tales of hell on earth / edited by Dan Kieran.–
1st Harper pbk. ed.
p.   cm.
ISBN-10: 0-06-083342-4
ISBN-13: 978-0-06-083342-8
1. Travel–Anecdotes.   2. Travel–Humor.   I. Kieran, Dan.
G151.I53 2006
910.4–dc22
2005054548

06   07   08   09   10   RRD   10   9   8   7   6   5   4   3   2   1

I don't want a holiday in the sun.

The Sex Pistols

Compiled and Edited by
Dan Kieran

Designed by
Sonia Ortiz Alcón

Illustrations by
Gwyn

Photographs by
Rita Kieran

Special thanks to Rachel and Wilfie

Acknowledgments:

Simon Benham, Brenda Kimber, Patrick Janson-Smith, Judith Welsh, Alison Tulett,
Emma Dowson, Claire Ward, Stephen Mulcahey, Fredrik Nordbeck, Tricia, Michael, Kelly
and everyone at Tourism Concern, Mathew Clayton, Chris Yates, Kevin Parr,
Henry Littlechild, Ben Hassett, Agnieska Debska, Kevin Kieran, Jill Kieran, Gareth Kieran,
Molly Smith, Roger Halton, Judy Munday, Ben Munday, Kit Munday, Nick Munday,
Richard Munday, Hugh Breton, Jo Mayer, Kieran Topping, Jamie Dwelly, Sylvie Poulton,
Gail and Brian, Lucy Poulton, James Poulton, Paul Hamilton, Will Hogan, Ian Vince,
Matthew DeAbaitua, Victoria Hull, Lawrence Pointer, John Frusciante, Elizabeth Wigmore,
The Three Bills, Pat Dennison, Mr. Chittock, Tom Espley, Ken MacKinnon, John Potter
and Colin Charde.

CRAP VACATIONS CONTENTS

HAVE YOU GOT THE BOOK 'CRAP VACATIONS'? THIS YEAR ME AND THE WIFE ARE GOING TO PLAN OUR TWO WEEKS IN THE SUN USING A LITTLE REVERSE PSYCHOLOGY
BOOK SHOP
GWYN

Travel agents tell us that the annual summer vacation is the perfect antidote to the stresses and strains of modern life. Throughout the year pictures of palm trees taunt us from the pages of newspapers and magazines while billboards of sun-drenched beaches mock us in the January rain. So when August finally arrives we dutifully hand over our credit card details and make the pilgrimage to the airport and on to foreign climes.

But what the brochures and the adverts don't tell us is that when we get home from our two weeks in the sun we're often more in need of a vacation than when we left. Whether it's transport delays, hotel disasters, stomach-churning food poisoning or family arguments, events tend to conspire to turn our vacation into a nightmare. In truth, modern vacations are like drugs. They cost a fortune and destroy families. And even if the immediate hit does feel strangely alluring, once you're back at home the come-down inevitably starts to kick in. You return to the office and find your desk has disappeared under an enormous backlog of work. And just when you think you've got through the worst of it your credit card bill arrives, which you have to pay off before embarking on the work/vacation treadmill for another year.

So when we put out a call for Crap Vacation stories to our readers, the *Idler* Web site was again bombarded with brilliant stories. The funniest and most surprising are published here. Overall it's a revealing snapshot of the huge disparity between what vacations promise and what they actually deliver. We've also included interesting and surprising snippets of vacation trivia, along with more savagely honest cartoons from the inimitable Gwyn.

By way of contrast, while we were compiling the book, we approached Tourism Concern, the only major charity working for fair and ethical conditions for the people who tend to us while we're on our well-deserved breaks. It seems that because we're so often exhausted from the trials of our daily jobs our sense of morality vanishes when it comes to going on vacation. We all need time to take it easy, but too often our leisure comes at someone else's expense. Thanks to the research of Tourism Concern we can reveal the five most ecologically damaging, dangerous and immoral vacation destinations on earth. These are just some of the places we unwittingly trample through in our quest for a life after work.

DAN KIERAN

50 STAG WEEK IN KAVOS, GREECE

STRESS	💩💩💩💩 ·
SICKNESS	💩 · · · ·
BOREDOM	💩💩💩 · ·
DANGER	💩💩💩 · ·
EXPLOITATION	💩💩💩 · ·

Duration: 7 days
Cost: $885

Before I start, whatever happened to the stag night? How come it's become a week's holiday these days? Just for the record, if you're getting married and want to celebrate the end of your freedom, go to a nightclub and order a stripper like people used to do in the old days. No one wants to go on a stag week. We've got better things to spend our limited vacation time and money on but we're too polite to say so, OK?

Anyway, back to the story. At the airport the T-shirts were handed out, which was

the first indication that the books I'd packed into my case could turn out to be superfluous pieces of luggage. The best man, Richard, had printed 'hilarious' slogans on each of our shirts. Mine said 'Sad Dad' on the front (on account of my sobering family life and the fact that I wasn't still going out taking pills every Friday night) and 'Dave's Stag, Kavos, 1999' emblazoned on the back. I was informed that my job for the week was to stop trying to persuade other people not to start drinking at 9 a.m. in the morning, which was, Richard reminded me, the whole point of our trip. Next he dished one out to 'Belcher'. His job was to belch as much as possible in inappropriate situations and into every microphone in every nightclub we visited. Then there was 'Shagger'—yes, you guessed it, he was single and therefore had to try and shag as many women as possible. Next to him there was 'Mincer' who was a trifle overweight and hadn't been that prolific with the ladies since we left school, leading to the masterful and hilarious deduction that he was, in fact, gay. His T-shirt was pink just to humiliate him even further. He was told to make sure he was always standing next to Dave to keep him out of trouble. Richard confided in me later that this wasn't to protect Dave but so that Dave would always look good in comparison when we were 'hunting the dago tarts in the clubs'. I resisted the urge to inform him that his racism was mis-

placed because we were, in fact, going to Greece rather than Spain but decided it would fall on somewhat deaf ears. The stag himself (my oldest, closest pal, Dave) just had 'The Stag' printed on his shirt, although he had an extra line on the back that declared, 'Please shag me, it's my last chance.' Meanwhile Simon, the show-off of the group whom everyone secretly hated even when we were at school, laughed smugly when he was given his shirt with 'The Dude' printed on the front. There's always one of your mates who doesn't get the piss taken out of him, isn't there? He's always a right wanker. Finally, Richard revealed his own shirt, which said simply, 'The Best Man.' We were ordered to strip off and put our T-shirts on before being frog-marched to the bar, where Richard had soon lined up seven pints of Stella with whiskey chasers. People literally parted in fear as we approached, an uncanny prediction of the week ahead. By the time I got onto the plane I felt sick. By the time I'd got off it I had been sick, several times. Cue much laughter from my 'pals' who were so relieved that someone else had made a fool of themselves first that they all stuck the boot in heartily like the weak-willed bullies most of us become in such situations. This torment continued throughout the week. I could drone on forever about the misery of that experience but will instead pick out a few highlights. 'Belcher' decided to spend the week trying to shag the fattest and ugliest woman he could find because he'd once seen a Web site based on this concept at work. Apparently it was the funniest thing he'd ever seen. I must say he outdid himself, notching up six complete howlers before we got home. 'The Stag' seemed to be in a state of constant torment as he was paraded and humiliated in front of loud women from England's less salubrious towns and cities. He told me some months later that it was one of the worst experiences of his life. 'Mincer' nearly drowned in the sea after being goaded by Richard into swimming immediately after he'd been persuaded to take thirteen consecutive blowbacks on a joint made with particularly potent skunk. 'Shagger' was notable only for the amount of Gut-buster breakfasts he managed to wolf down at the Eastenders (I kid you not) Café. 'The Dude' shagged two of the most beautiful, bikini-clad women I've ever seen, all the while revelling in everyone else's misfortune. 'Sad Dad' and 'The Best Man', meanwhile, had a curious conversation on the final night where he confided to me that his regular Ecstasy use had put him on the verge of schizophrenia. 'I know you won't believe it,' he said earnestly, half an hour after trying to whip me in the testicles with a wet towel, 'but I'm manically depressed.'

He then offered me some Prozac, before making a startling statement that I still can't quite believe. 'It works straight away if you snort it.'

ANON

VACATION STDS

• Between 2000 and 2002 69% of men in the UK infected with HIV contracted the disease while they were abroad.

• 20% of syphilis cases in men are contracted while abroad.

49 CRUISE TO THE BAHAMAS

Duration: 8 days
Cost: $855

I was forced to go on a family holiday to Florida so that I could meet my sister's new fiancé. We're not really that close but as it was Thanksgiving and I had the time off from school I figured, what the hell.

On day two someone had the great idea to take a day cruise to the Bahamas. We arrived at the ship early and had a disappointing breakfast. As it pulled away from the dock I noticed a woman in trouble out of the corner of my eye. She was about seventy and was trying to carry a tray of badly cooked eggs and coffee. I turned to watch her, wondering if I should help, but before I could get up she tumbled

'MY SHIRT HAD BEEN COVERED
IN A PUTRID LAYER OF BILE'

about fifteen feet down the aisle and landed on her face. It was only then that I noticed that we were about half a mile out to sea and it was already getting pretty rough. My soon-to-be brother-in-law—we'll call him Steve—and I decided to go out on deck and get a good seat near the railings, just in case. We found a great spot on some sun-loungers and tried not to think about the up and down motion—land there one minute and nothing but waves the next. All of a sudden the wind really picked up and a big spray hit us both. For a moment I didn't realize what had happened but then I noticed that poor Steve had someone's partially digested breakfast in his hair while my shirt had been covered in a layer of putrid bile. It just got worse from there and within an hour everyone was sick. The railings were crowded with passengers puking into the sea. I decided to venture indoors. What a mistake. The only people still inside were those passengers too ill, old or disabled to make it out on deck. Even the crew were puking in the toilets, then cleaning a bit, then puking some more. Vomit sloshed around the corridors in waves.

This was too much for me and I resigned myself to my previous fate. I took my place on the railings next to a family and emptied the contents of my stomach into the sea, over and over again. And I don't normally join in on the group activities. After an hour of this, and with stomach muscle exhaustion setting in, I decided to find the rest of my family. I searched for ages but one person bent over a ship's railings looks very much like another. I eventually found my mother. She had managed to nab one of the bins for her own private use. It was about a quarter full. I just hoped it wasn't all hers.

Finally we landed in Nassau and it was heaven to be on solid earth again. The time passed very quickly and soon we were boarding for the return journey, which was uneventful, thank God.

DANIEL

48 NEWQUAY, ENGLAND

STRESS	💩	💩	•	•	•
SICKNESS	💩	•	•	•	•
BOREDOM	💩	💩	💩	•	•
DANGER	💩	💩	💩	•	•
EXPLOITATION	💩	•	•	•	•

Duration: N/A
Cost: N/A

Once upon a time Newquay was a sleepy fishing village that had some of the best surf spots in the country. That was then. Now you will find it promoted by the *Sun* newspaper as the 'Ibiza of the UK'.

Go midsummer or on any bank holiday and you will find a town overrun by illiterate morons, trashed on a concoction of scrumpy cider and as many illegal substances as their bodies will hold, all the while slurring obscenities at any member of the opposite sex who crosses their path. If

GWYN

you can find a space on the beach it is likely to be littered with used condoms and empty McDonald's burger boxes and God forbid you try surfing these legendary waters: again you will be assailed with sewage and joined by thousands of people who cram themselves into the sea leaving only space for a small five-year-old. Nighttime brings out the lager louts, prostitutes, drug dealers and vampires who swarm on the streets *en masse* and pile into these extortionately priced dens of iniquity commonly known as nightclubs. Newquay was once a place of relaxation, now it's just a place of desperation where brides and grooms to be gather for their last nights of freedom and debauchery. It says something when the local people leave during the summer. **JAMES**

47 SNOWBOARDING IN SWEDEN

STRESS	💩	💩	💩	·	·
SICKNESS	💩	·	·	·	·
BOREDOM	💩	💩	💩	💩	💩
DANGER	💩	💩	💩	·	·
EXPLOITATION	·	·	·	·	·

Duration: 3 days
Cost: Nothing

An unfaithful ex-boyfriend had persuaded me to go on a 'get-back-together' trip to Sweden in an attempt to win back my favour. Either that or he had no one else to go with. The only interruption to our snowflake–fallen idyll would be his DJ-ing at a trip-hop festival for...the entire weekend. How wrong that reads now.

The hotel lobby was damply chilled and uninspiring. My spirits rose when they handed us our all-expenses-paid weekend ski passes but things began to go downhill, pardon the pun, when I noticed that it wasn't my name on the laminate I'd been handed but the name of the girl he had recently been seeing behind my back. We ended the evening quietly bickering in a silent dining room that had been brutally carved from one piece of dark wood, surrounded by German DJs and their girlfriends.

The next morning I set off excitedly for the promised free snowboarding with...let's call him James. It quickly transpired that James had sorted himself out with a cutting-edge outfit of the highest technical and sartorial standards prior to the trip, whilst I was palmed off with a fleece jester's hat and an XXL purple suit borrowed from one of his new mates. I couldn't see a thing, but this wasn't what stopped my fun, no, it was the blizzard that did that. When the second James stood up on his board he slipped

theatrically and landed on his arse as his board completely disappeared into the snow. Then, while we waited for the instructor to rescue it the mountain was evacuated because of the bad weather. James wasn't too pleased.

Later that night, another silent cab journey took us to the 4,000-capacity tent where we found twenty German boys in bad shoes throwing beer cans at Beck. The main act hadn't turned up and the mood was steaming, despite the brutal cold. James began very, very small talk

'I WAS PALMED OFF WITH A FLEECE JESTER'S HAT'

17

with an ancient Norwegian techno lord before embarking on his mammoth seven-hour set. I was left to walk alone around the freezing circus tent with nothing to keep me warm except my steadily increasing rage. After spending hours and hours being miserably pounded into oblivion by strobe lights and bad fashion with nothing to do but stare at my own freezing breath, the music finally stopped. It then transpired that the dancing audience (five people) had inadvertently covered all the records with a fine layer of sawdust. The drama that ensued was something to behold 'Look...at...this...' James mouthed to his DJ pal (the laughably titled 'Partner in Crhyme') as he held his records up in the flickering light. The pontification was really something to behold (I mean for fuck's sake, any fool could see all you had to do was blow). I gently interjected that we were about to miss the last cab only to be met with a torrent of abuse. It was the only conversation I'd had all night.

Once back in the hotel room a different kind of silence descended as James 'chanced' upon a porn channel. He looked at me suggestively.

I glared at him. 'No.'

RACHEL DEVINE

46 CUBA, ALL-INCLUSIVE

STRESS	💩	💩	💩	💩	·
SICKNESS	💩	·	·	·	·
BOREDOM	💩	💩	💩	·	·
DANGER	💩	💩	💩	·	·
EXPLOITATION	💩	💩	💩	💩	💩

Duration: 1 week
Cost: ¢710

For months I'd been looking forward to a seven-day, all-inclusive vacation with two mates. A week spent boozing by the beach; smoking cigars with the odd excursion into groovy Havana...err, right.

We arrived at the hotel and were immediately advised to remain within the confines of the complex for the entire vacation and not to go out into the country itself. This was a far cry from the sun-bleached retro Cadillacs that had been gliding through the streets of my imagination. As it happened, the brochure had deceived us anyway and we were miles from Havana, fucking typical.

The hotel had its own private beach, which was fenced off from the locals and patrolled by armed guards. Alarmed as to why we needed armed guards I asked one of the barmen why they were there. 'To stop the locals hassling you for money and ruining your vacation,' he replied. It was nice to be vacationing at the sharp end of global, financial apartheid then. I didn't remember seeing that advertised in the brochure. I spent the rest of the vacation wrung out with guilt and seething self-loathing. Still, I suppose it was an unusually honest example of the whole, 'western holidaymaker lives like a king for fuck-all money in the financially crippled developing world his country has created through the protectionism and racketeering that passes for global free trade'.

Christ, that vacation turned me into a fucking hippie, now that definitely wasn't mentioned in the brochure.

CHAD

45 VENICE EN QUEBEC, CANADA

STRESS	💩 💩 💩 💩 •
SICKNESS	• • • • •
BOREDOM	💩 • • • •
DANGER	💩 💩 💩 • •
EXPLOITATION	• • • • •

Duration: 1 week
Cost: $880

When our daughter was about three, my wife and I decided it would be fun to spend a week in a small cabin on the shores of New York State's Lake Champlain. We live in Ottawa, so the plan was to have a rela-tively inexpensive vacation that would allow time for leisure, swimming and a couple of zoo visits to view wildlife our daughter had only previously seen in books. Because we had boundless faith in both the Web site's description of the resort and the verbal promises of a cheerful helper at the host town's Chamber of Commerce, I paid up front and booked us into the cabin for a week. We were staying in a place with a charmingly rus-tic name (that I will not mention for legal rea-sons) in the town of Venice en Quebec, perched atop the one tiny finger of Lake Champlain that juts out of New York State into Canadian territory.

After a couple of hours on the road from Ottawa we got to the town and passed a roadside bar whose parking lot was filled with about twenty evil-looking black Harley-Davidsons. These scary-looking machines were surrounded by dozens of bikers all

THE APOCALYPSE NOW TOUR · Movie buffs can now relive some of the highlights of Francis Ford Coppola's classic film *Apocalypse Now* with a tour operator called Wild Frontiers. Its Web site proclaims, 'Charlie don't surf, but you can! Up river into the Heart of Darkness; water-ski to the Stones behind a speedboat; dinner party at a French 1930s colonial plantation; and ride in a helicopter over the palm trees and paddy fields while listening to the *March of the Valkyries*.' But this hilarious re-enactment of the search for Colonel Kurtz is lost on some of the locals. Helicopters swooping overhead have brought back memories of napalm and mass slaughter that they would rather forget.

CRAP VACATION TRIVIA

UNSPOILED RUSTIC CHARM

wearing soiled black leather. I gulped and drove on with increasing trepidation.

Our chalet turned out to be one in a line of shed-like structures that resembled the abandoned outhouses that littered the horizon after the nuclear disaster in Chernobyl. The 'beach' was an oil-slicked boat-launch ramp across an exceedingly busy roadway. The 'pool' was essentially a large, dirty paddling pool that stood four feet off the ground. As we headed into the office to register, we watched as some slob stood atop a minuscule poolside diving platform, chewed the last few kernels from his heavily buttered cob of corn, tossed it onto the grass and then toppled into the water. Thoughtfully, he left his half-consumed bottle of beer on the platform.

I don't even know why we unpacked. But we did and, about fifteen minutes later, someone opened the double doors of an actual garage (the kind for cars) that lay just across the driveway from our chalet, revealing two columns of massive stereo speakers. The next thing we knew, our one tiny window started vibrating as the near-deafening strains of Billy Ray Cyrus's 'Achy Breaky Heart' finally pummelled us into submission. I took the cabin key, walked back into the office, mumbled something about a family emergency, asked the owner to send us any money he thought fair if he was able to re-rent our hastily vacated chalet (no prizes for guessing how much we received), packed the car and family and drove back home. Still, we could look forward to a scenic drive home. According to a guide-book one route home would take us through Akwesasne, a First Nations reservation straddling the Canada/US border. This turned out to be another anticlimax. The view was rather spoiled by the huge flags on every second house proclaiming, 'You are on Mohawk Warrior Land!'

Once safely back in Ontario we stopped at a convenience store and our toddler was beside herself with pleasure as she sat on a tiny patch of lawn eating a choc-ice, while my wife and I agreed that we'd just go home and spend the week day-tripping out of the house. **ANON**

44 SOUTH DEVON, ENGLAND

STRESS	💩	💩	💩	💩	•
SICKNESS	💩	💩	💩	•	•
BOREDOM	💩	💩	•	•	•
DANGER	💩	💩	💩	💩	•
EXPLOITATION	•	•	•	•	•

Duration: 1 week
Cost: $580

I spent a cheerless and charm-free week in South Devon with the rest of my family when I was nine. It quickly became not only one of the most surreal but also the most terrifying vacations of my life. We were staying in a shed. (It was called a chalet, but actually it was a wooden shed about the size of a small garage.) The whole thing was mysteriously mounted on train wheels and parked in a field with about thirty others, all painted bright and breezy colours, yet all uniformly

KINGSBRIDGE-SOUTH DEVON

incompatible with fun. In each, there were enough beds, though not enough room, for four people to not quite get on with one another. It turned out to be perfect accommodation for a family to lose their minds while on the run from creditors.

But before we could crumple into insanity, there was my asthma to contend with. It was my worst year for it ever. I managed to have three serious attacks that week and the strain probably didn't help matters along. Once we were up on the moors, however, the asthma disappeared—to make room for a series of volcanic and unreasonable family arguments, including one about tomato ketchup that must have had a darker subtext, as it ended with my mother smashing plates in the back of our Vauxhall Viva Estate. Another involved finding a mutilated sheep (surely some kind of metaphysical statement about family love), while my father became incandescent with rage about a slim, possibly self-published, book of *Exmoor Family Walks* and its less than comprehensive directions. We left in uneasy silence after an afternoon of anger and loathing, low blood sugar and disorientation, having torn a tangible psychic rip through Lorna Doone Country. I've not been back.

IAN VINCE

CRAP VACATION TRIVIA

• Despite being nestled in one of the most beautiful parts of Britain, the beach at Combe Martin, in Devon, was recently named as one of the dirtiest in Britain.

43 FINDHORN, SCOTLAND

STRESS	💩	💩	💩	💩	💩
SICKNESS	💩	•	•	•	•
BOREDOM	💩	💩	💩	💩	💩
DANGER	💩	•	•	•	•
EXPLOITATION	💩	💩	•	•	•

Duration: 48 hours
Cost: Nothing

Looking back, going camping in Scotland for a vacation was perhaps a bit naive, but this wasn't any ordinary campsite. It was a campsite beside a hippie commune in a place called Findhorn, which is located right next to an American Air Force base on the edge of the Moray Firth. I felt slightly bewildered as I pitched my tent while a flock of B52 bombers lifted off the runway that ended a few hundred yards from where I was hoping to sleep, but was intrigued by the enormous greenhouse that lay a few yards away. This intrigue gave way to stomach-churning panic when I discovered the greenhouse was, in fact, 'A Living Toilet'. Eco-toilet my arse. It was just a big hole in the ground filled with hippie excrement and sawdust, covered by a poly tunnel. When the wind blew in from the east (all day every day) it was like staying in a shit-filled turbine on the coast of hell. After a sleepless first night harangued by nightmares (involving fighter planes, burning turds and my tent) I headed for the commune reception area to sign in. The commune actively encouraged visitors. In exchange for a morning's work you were fed and grinned at by purple-trouser-wearing middle-aged women recovering from nervous breakdowns. You may ask what the hell I was doing there. It's a bloody good question. I blame a particularly nasty relationship break-up and too many Sundays watching the Food Network. I opted to work in the garden and headed for the rows and rows of vegetables on the other side of the grounds. There were six of us in all, but I was the only 'volunteer'. The lady who ran the garden was an attractive American woman who spoke to us as though we were a bunch of five-year-olds. She instructed us to hold hands in a circle so we could 'bless the garden' before asking each of us in turn to imagine that we were a tree. After imagining this for a while, and swaying from side to side humming, she asked

help! Please, will you come and help me?' The other four slipped off and I found myself being led around the garden with a hoe in my hand. Before starting work she held my wrists, looked into my eyes and said, 'Don't forget to

us to explain to the group which kind of tree we were. After confessing that she was an oak tree, the other three turned out to be pine trees and then I too confirmed that I was an oak tree. The American woman grinned at me and asked if anyone needed my help with their morning's work. I looked around the circle, expecting some kind of response, but they all just stared at their feet, looking full of guilt. She turned back to me and smiled nervously. 'That's great! I need

thank the weeds when you pull them out of the ground. Thank them for doing their job in the garden, then place them carefully over there.' She pointed at a compost heap. 'Then they can live again in the earth.' I had been idly nursing the vague hope of a shag and a decent bed for the night, but she appeared to be completely and utterly insane. I had intended to stay for a week, but then the rain came. I wept in my tent for the next twelve hours, tortured by the never-ending drone of warplanes and the numbing cold of a Scottish summer night. The next morning I picked up the remaining pieces of my fractured spirit and left.

DAN KIERAN

42 RHODES, GREECE

STRESS	💩💩💩 · ·	
SICKNESS	💩💩 · · ·	
BOREDOM	💩💩 · · ·	
DANGER	💩💩 · · ·	
EXPLOITATION	💩💩 · · ·	

Duration: 2 weeks
Cost: €590

The island of Rhodes stinks of shit. The food is overpriced and tastes revolting. The local beer is awful. Most of the island's architecture is half finished (to avoid tax, which is only due on completed properties) and covered in bird excrement. Local flora and fauna consist of lizards and scrub coated in motor oil. Worst of all is Faliraki, which nightly fills with the grunts of a thousand drunken women being roughly butt-fucked by disease-addled strangers. I'd rather eat my own feces than ever visit Rhodes again.   **BEN**

LUXURY RIVERSIDE APARTMENT

41 STONEHENGE, ENGLAND

STRESS					
SICKNESS					
BOREDOM					
DANGER					
EXPLOITATION					

Duration: 24 hours
Cost: ¢175

The lady in Salisbury's tourist office confirmed to me that Stonehenge was one of the most important sites for me and my girlfriend, both travelling Americans, to see during our three-week trek around the UK. I had planned to propose at the site of the ruin. I had read something about its ancient mystical properties and my beloved, a crystal-wearing hippie, was sure to cry with joy as I fell to my knees and asked her the question of all questions in the shadow of one of the world's most impor-

tant sites of antiquity. It would cost $26 to get a taxi there from Salisbury and a further $100 to stay in a local hotel intriguingly titled a 'Travelodge' that was within walking distance of the ancient monument. Now, the UK's expensive at the best of times and this was seriously pushing my budget; still, it was a big occasion so I decided to splash out. I had a vague, romantic idea of the sun setting over a log cabin perched on the downs within site of Stonehenge. Milly and I lying in each other's arms, the ring I'd bought, sitting comfortably on her finger. So we got in a taxi and headed for our hotel. Anyone who's visited Stonehenge will now be laughing heartily at my naive misfortune. Suffice to say 'walking distance' meant a forty-five-minute hike alongside a freeway. And the 'Travelodge' was some kind of soulless flytrap for depressed travelling salesmen. Imagine Jack Lemmon in *Glengarry Glen Ross* and you're talking salesman of the month in this hopeless hellhole that was stuck in the parking lot of a gas station. Our room, inevitably, was right next to the deafening road. Hoping to salvage something from the situation I enquired about the possibility of room service while Milly shifted uneasily from one foot to another on the stained, grey carpet. The old hag behind the counter shook her head and muttered something about a 'Little Chef' while pointing to an adjoining building. This 'restau-

WHAT DO THE RUNES SAY OF THE GLORIOUS FUTURE OF OUR MAGNIFICENT STONE HENGE?
I SEE A TRAVEL LODGE ....AND A.... LITTLE CHEF
GWYN

rant' was like Wendy's but six times as expensive and without the charm or class. Not quite the romantic venue I'd been hoping for. Still, I tried to put a brave face on it. There was our visit to the monument itself the following day; at least that would make up for everything. We got up early and made our way on foot towards the ancient ruin. After about half an hour it started to rain. The kind of life-sapping rain you only get in the UK. Milly fell over in the mud and somewhere on the journey lost one of her 'life' crystals. We spent an hour retracing our steps in the freezing rain until we'd located it. She cried with joy on finding it only for a juggernaut to hurtle past and sweep the pair of us into a thorny hodge. Her bedraggled purple hair and tie-dye trousers stuck to her shivering, now bleeding, frame as we trekked the final kilometre to the ancient ruin. And then things took a turn for the worse. After ten minutes wandering round the fenced-off collection of stones there is nothing much left to see. I mean it's impressive, kind of, but once you've looked at it from six different views there's fuck all else to do. It's crap. It's just a load of stones between a fork in the road. I couldn't quite summon the guts to propose in the immediate vicinity of a freeway whilst being gawped at by a troop of bored tourists. We made our way back to the Travelodge in silence. There must have been something in the air between the prefabricated

paper-thin walls because as soon as we got back we had a horrendous argument that was quickly followed by a tortuous dinner. Needless to say the food was expensive and fucking horrible. Milly had putrid maple syrup pancakes because she didn't like the vegetarian option and the burger I ordered was so greasy and tasteless I didn't realize I'd eaten most of the fat-drenched napkin it had been resting on when I came to the end of my meal. Milly laughed cruelly and said it was the perfect metaphor for our relationship (which, incidentally, I still don't understand). We broke up when we got back to Newark airport a few days later. Fuck you, Stonehenge.

GREG

THE FIVE MOST ECOLOGICALLY DAMAGING VACATIONS ON EARTH

When we get away from it all we all want a destination that's off the beaten track, unspoiled by the tourist hordes and somewhere we can truly relax. Of course all vacation destinations were once like that. Until the developers and the tourists arrived...

5 THE GALÁPAGOS ISLANDS

In 1995 the Ecuadorian government allowed tourist numbers to the Galápagos Islands to triple from 20,000 to 60,000 a year. This led to overcrowding in towns like Puerta Ayora, where Ecuadorians flocked to take advantage of the booming tourist industry. The additional workers brought their families and their animals—cats, dogs and goats, none of which were endemic to the islands. These animals often escaped, became feral, mated and competed with local animals for food. Feral cats and dogs began eating iguanas and tortoises. But it's not just the workers who've had an effect on the local wildlife. The number of giant tortoises has fallen dramatically after scientists began inseminating the females to try and bolster the declining population. Now the females prefer the artificial method to the natural one, male giant tortoises being notoriously lazy, so the numbers are reducing even further. And then there are the growing number of cruise liners coming to the Galápagos Islands. These boats routinely empty raw sewage into the sea within fifteen miles of the shore, destroying marine life. They are also blamed for the huge increase in litter that has begun washing up daily on the islands' shores. Add to this the increase in fishing trips, day-trippers, jet skiers and helicopter flights and the future for the Galápagos Islands began to look rather bleak. However, the Ecuadorian government has taken notice. New laws are planned to restrict migration and to increase the strictness of cargo inspection. They are also resisting pressure from tour operators to increase the number of tourists and the size of many tour boats. While it seems that the Galápagos Islands are turning a corner, the best thing you can do to help preserve them for generations to come is not to go there at all. David Attenborough did a great programme about them with the BBC that you can buy on DVD.

4 CRUISES

Since 1970 the number of people going on cruises has increased by 1,000%. According to Ross A. Klein, author of *Cruise Ship Blues,* 'a typical cruise ship with 2,600 passengers on a one-week voyage produces on average: 245,000 gallons of sewage, 2.2 million gallons of grey water, 37,000 gallons of oily bilge water, 141 gallons of photo chemicals, seven gallons of dry-cleaning waste, thirteen gallons of used paints, five pounds of batteries, ten pounds of fluorescent lights, three pounds of medical waste, and 108 pounds of expired chemicals', most of which just gets dumped into the sea. The extent of illegal pollution caused by cruise liners is unknown, but Royal Caribbean Ltd were recently found guilty of 'a fleet-wide conspiracy to use the United States waterways as its dumping ground'. According to the inspectors, 'Ships were rigged with secret piping systems to bypass pollution treatment equipment.' Royal Caribbean Ltd pled guilty and was fined a record $18 million.

3 GOLF VACATIONS

The GAGM (the Global Anti-Golf Movement) campaigns against golf. Not because golfers are pretentious or rude, have stupid rules about certain types of hats, discriminate against women and behave with insufferable smugness, but because golf course developments are catastrophic for the environment. According to the *Defence of Nature and the Environment*, a golf course in Spain consumes the same amount of water in ten hours that 8,640 people would in an entire day. In Australia a golf course is being planned in the desert that will use an estimated one million cubic metres of water every year. Clean water is the most precious resource on earth. One billion people in the world today do not have access to it, and it is estimated that a child dies every fifteen seconds of disease caused by a lack of clean water or sanitation. It is because of this that in the developing world golf courses have become a symbol of western exploitation and waste. Golf courses are also, not unnaturally, unpopular with people who get evicted to make way for them. In Hawaii golf courses have sprung up in some of the most beautiful parts of the island, one of which involved bulldozing a sacred native burial site. In Mexico a protestor was shot and killed by supporters of a golf course development, three others were imprisoned and eleven more arrested because they opposed the building of the 18-hole golf course complex that included a five-star hotel, business park and a helicopter pad. In the Philippines 10,000 farmers were forcibly evicted from their land to make way for a golf course development. In the protest that followed two farmers were killed by the Philippine army.

THE SUPER RESORTS

The future of tourism lies with the super resort. These are vast, million-dollar projects built on fragile ecosystems that defy both logic and imagination to cater for the whims of the super rich. Even if you've run out of prime real estate on your shoreline all you have to do is dump thousands of tons of rock into the ocean and you too can build your own man-made island paradise.

DUBAI—Using its vast wealth, Dubai has great plans to transform itself into the top tourist destination in the world. Here are their most ambitious billion-dollar projects:
• **THE WORLD**—Made up of 300 man-made islands ranging in size from 250,000–900,000 sq feet, the entire development is nine kilometres long and six kilometres wide.
• **THE PALM ISLANDS**—Three man-made islands have been built off the coast of Dubai in the shape of palm trees. Collectively they will provide sixty luxury hotels, countless shopping centres, six marinas, a 'Sea Village', a water theme park, health spas, cinemas, houses built on stilts, holiday apartments, villas, private homes and 'water apartments'.
• **WATERWORLD**—A mecca for shoppers, Waterworld will cover nine million square feet and include a shopping mall the size of fifty football fields, a 4.3-million-square-foot artificial lake and parking for 16,000 cars.

INDIA—India has lagged behind the world when it comes to luxury tourist developments. Until now.
• **THE SUNDARBANS**—The world's largest delta area situated in West Bengal is a World Heritage Site. A project on land and sea worth $155 million is being planned to build a five-star floating hotel complex, a golf course, casinos, helipads, shopping centres and restaurants. Local people are worried the development will force them from their land, destroy their local environment and decimate one of the largest remaining concentrations of tigers left in India.

THE NEW DUBAI

THE OLD DUBAI

1 ANYWHERE IN AN AIRPLANE

Today the pollution caused by air travel is highlighted so often, and in such bizarre ways (see page 37) that the figures become increasingly absurd and meaningless to the average holidaymaker. This suits most of us down to the ground. No one wants to feel guilty about the environmental damage caused to the planet by getting on an airplane. Frankly we haven't got the time.

The average UK worker gets a paltry four-week vacation a year. In Britain we work the longest hours in Europe, and a recent study found that a medieval peasant worked less than the average American. With Gordon Brown's recent opt-out of the European forty-eight-hour working week, Britain is now firmly on the path of the workaholic economic model of the US (where just two weeks annual vacation is the norm).

You can hardly blame people who get so little leisure time for not being interested in the environmental impact of getting in a plane a couple of times a year. The ice-caps, meanwhile, continue to melt at an alarming speed.

In the not too distant future, when retirement is nothing but a vague memory from a bygone era, the stakes will be raised even further as the annual vacation becomes the only time in our lives when we get to relax. The tourist industry is already the biggest in the world and accounts for 8.6% of jobs worldwide. Low-cost airlines and plans to increase capacity in the UK's airports, despite the government's claims about an interest in slowing down global warming, mean that in the years to come the environmental damage to the planet caused by aviation will escalate beyond the green movement's worst fears. Socrates said that people who work too hard don't have the time to fulfil their responsibilities as citizens. In the West we have become too busy working to consider the environmental cost of how we spend our precious leisure time. To save the planet from a literal global meltdown we'll have to start by addressing our intoxication with overwork and overconsumption.

Perhaps then the publication of scientific facts about imminent environmental catastrophe won't be met with the sound of millions of heads being buried in the sand.

ECO-UNFRIENDLY FACTS AND FIGURES

The greenhouse gas emitted per passenger on a return flight from London to Amsterdam is the same as the weight of 179 Edam cheeses.

Each passenger's share of the pollution caused by a return flight from London to Florida is the same as the pollution created by the average motorist in a year.

A mini driving round the earth 640 times creates as much carbon per passenger as flying to Sydney from the UK.

Emissions at altitude have 2.7 times the environmental impact of those on the ground.

50% of the UK population flew at least once in 2001.

Unlike car drivers, the aviation industry doesn't have to pay tax or VAT on fuel. According to HM Customs this equates to an effective subsidy of £5 billion per year.

According to *Green Futures* magazine, air passenger numbers are set to double by 2020 and treble by 2030.

Aircraft emissions were excluded from the Kyoto protocol.

SOURCE: The *Independent*

40 SAILING IN GREECE

STRESS	💩	💩	•	•	•
SICKNESS	💩	•	•	•	•
BOREDOM	💩	💩	💩	💩	💩
DANGER	💩	💩	💩	•	•
EXPLOITATION	•	•	•	•	•

Duration: 2 weeks
Cost: Nothing

If there's one thing more beautiful than Greece it's the sea and the islands around it. Or so you would think. In August it's blissfully hot and you are guaranteed fabulous weather. Hmm. Sailing itself is challenging, but still fun.

Yeah, right.

I was only fifteen, but it was my first proper foreign vacation, so naturally I was very excited. So were my parents, both of whom had just passed the sailing course that they needed to have completed

in order to hire the boat in the first place. Quite what we would have done if they'd failed I have no idea. If only we'd been lucky enough to find out.

The vacation consisted of effectively renting a boat for a fortnight. We were part of a flotilla that was sailing around the Greek Islands. You had the choice of following everyone else or going off and doing your own thing. My parents decided we should go off and do our own thing with a couple from Nottingham named Jason and Ange. I wanted to follow Claire and Robert from Liverpool and their daughter Jenny. I'd met her on the plane and lent her my tape of Poison's *Open Up and Say . . . Ahh!* But we didn't, and I only saw her once again briefly after that.

I got sunburnt on the second day, forgetting that you don't really feel your skin blistering in the light Mediterranean breeze. So I spent the rest of the vacation dowsing myself in aftersun lotion and covering up with a large baggy sweater and tracksuit trousers. This meant I was unable to go out in the sun, swim or do anything during daylight hours. If only the same could be said for Jason and Ange.

Jason and Ange turned out to be naturists. Which was quite off-putting for everyone else in the flotilla, whom I noticed seemed to be avoiding us like the plague. Jason was hung like a rhinoceros and Ange was shaved bare. Not the kind of accompaniment a virgin fifteen-year-old needs to see on vacation, but things, staggeringly, still managed to get worse. After two days, Jason and Ange managed to persuade my parents to try a bit of naturism themselves. Embarrassment isn't the word. Especially when Claire and Robert from Liverpool were about to moor alongside us. My nude mum, who had been bent over a coil of rope shouted, "Oh David, look, it's Jenny!" At which point Claire and Robert looked aghast, realized both my parents were naked and promptly sailed off again.

And then we got stuck in a storm.

Being on a sailboat in a storm with naked and now arguing parents was the last straw. After that I vowed never to go on a family vacation ever again.

DAVID LETISSIER

39 COACH TRIP TO ITALY

STRESS	💩 💩	· · ·
SICKNESS	💩 💩 💩	· ·
BOREDOM	💩 💩 💩 💩	·
DANGER	💩 💩 💩	· ·
EXPLOITATION	· · · · ·	

Duration: 1 week
Cost: €440

After a 4 a.m. start in the school car park in deepest west Wales we arrived in London. Despite the fact that the journey to Italy would take a bottom-numbing thirty-eight hours by coach, Mr Wigley decided that we should have a tour of the capital en route, as there was a terminally ill asthmatic girl on board who, due to the terminal nature of her condition, might not get to see it otherwise. Thereby adding an extra four hours to the already torturously long journey. So, we drove up the Mall, and saw Nelson's Column, but

the pièce de résistance was driving to Heathrow, parking up on a road that was 'quite near' the flight path and watching some airplanes take off and land, reminding us cruelly that we could actually be in Italy within two hours, were we not creeping across Europe in a bright-blue Shearings coach.

The first place we visited was Florence. We spent the day ambling round 'important sculptures' with hunched shoulders. The evening ended standing on Ponte Vecchio listening to Mr Wigley and Mrs Wyn, the music teacher, sing 'He's Got the Whole World in His Hands' with the hostel's resident happy-clappy German Evangelicals. Then it was on to Pompeii where my travelling companions staggered as far as the amphitheatre and spent all our free time bitching about the other girls on the trip. Desperate to experience more, but not allowed to go anywhere alone, I sat, impotent, under the shade of a cedar tree, watching another girl flapping her hand listlessly, moaning that it was 'too bloody 'ot'.

In Capri, we went no further than the junk-filled harbour. My companions lay on the pebble beach and got so sunburnt they blistered. I can still recall the pus-filled reptilian texture of one girl's back and another girl's repulsed face as she rubbed suncream on it. A case of closing the stable door after the horse has bolted if ever I saw it. The driver got lost on the way to Rome so in 104-degree heat we drove around the seedy suburbs of the Eternal City. People sprayed deodorant liberally, forcing Mr Wigley to proclaim that if one more person sprayed an aerosol we would go home immediately because it might kill the asthmatic girl. A trip to the Vatican had been organized, and the coach dropped us off. My travelling companions decided that no, they didn't really fancy looking 'at another fucking church' and promptly wandered off in search of Metallica T-shirts.

To top it all, the object of my devotion, Philip Dean, whose shorts-clad bottom I had followed open mouthed as we climbed up Vesuvius (misty, so no view and with hundreds of little black flies swarming about), copped off with a little minx from the second year.

E. ANGUS

38 CORNWALL, ENGLAND

STRESS	💩 💩 💩 · ·
SICKNESS	💩 💩 💩 · ·
BOREDOM	💩 💩 💩 · ·
DANGER	💩 💩 · · ·
EXPLOITATION	· · · · ·

Duration: 1 week
Cost: $140

When I was on my first summer break from university I'd been invited down to Cornwall by a girl I'd become friendly with in my hall of residence, the sort of girl I would have considered relationship material in the sixth form; so in the newly discovered grown-up atmosphere of university life I thought I was on for a week of uninhibited non-stop sex on the beach. I made the long train journey down to Cornwall in midsummer—it took a hell of a lot longer than I thought, but I was happy in my increasingly complicated and vivid erotic reverie. I got off the train to be met by the girl, plus her boyfriend, who turned out to be something with nuclear weapons in the Navy and bristling with a beard and leather motorbike jacket. I was taken to her mother's house, where I was introduced to her younger brother, a rabid vegetarian and Esperanto speaker who apparently had only revealed his homosexuality to his parents a few weeks before. Then I realized, the girl I'd been planning on shagging for a fortnight obviously thought I was gay and had planned the trip to set me up with her brother. His mother confided in me that he'd just been upstairs in front of the bathroom mirror trying on some new blue underwear that she had bought him before winking at me suggestively. I consequently spent a miserable week being driven around tourist sites in the back of a Datsun Sunny sandwiched between two militant expressions of virility. As a result I became very constipated.

ANON

37 AGADIR, MOROCCO

STRESS	🌀 🌀 🌀 · ·
SICKNESS	🌀 · · · ·
BOREDOM	🌀 🌀 🌀 · ·
DANGER	🌀 🌀 🌀 🌀 ·
EXPLOITATION	🌀 · · · ·

Duration: 2 weeks
Cost: $620

I had been looking forward to my two-week trip windsurfing in Agadir for ages. I had booked a package vacation because it meant that windsurfers and water-sport equipment would be available so I wouldn't need to drag them there.

The day before my departure I was telephoned by my travel agent and told the 'good' news. I had been upgraded to the best hotel in the area, which was a mile from the beach and had no windsurfing equipment. I was sufficiently vocal in my disappointment that arrangements were made for me to use the original hotel's facilities.

On the flight out I was wedged between the window and a very well-dressed, unfriendly man in a white suit. During the meal my miniature bottle of red wine rolled off the minute table and onto the man's lap. I apologetically fumbled around vainly trying to wipe the stain from his crotch. His shaking, red face led me to the conclusion that he was extremely upset. The rest of the flight was spent in a rather hostile atmosphere. His jacket and trousers were so stained that when we arrived in Agadir he was picked out by customs for questioning as he looked like a drunken loser on a stag night.

When I got to my smart hotel I was told by the staff that under no circumstances should I walk directly across the sand dunes to the other hotel, whose kicking nightlife was tauntingly within earshot, but to walk another mile on the road that led round to it instead. I ignored their patronizing advice and immediately set off directly across the sand dunes. I had hardly walked for five minutes before I realized I was being followed by a group of men. After the warning from the hotel staff I began to feel like a real arse. Then it became obvious there were even more men in the dunes in front of me. With a pounding heart I changed direction and noticed that even more men were closing in. Soon I was surrounded and, sweating profusely, awaited their attack. The sand dunes, it turned out, were a notorious local cruising spot. To my amazement several of them dropped their trousers and began masturbating furiously, gesturing for me to join in. I turned and ran through the sand.

I saw the white-suited man back at the hotel later and for the rest of the trip he seemed to be tailing me, frowning in my direction and muttering unpleasantries about me to the hotel staff. He obviously didn't want me around but of course there was nowhere else for me to go. The nightlife was nonexistent. Strolling out at night to the other hotel resulted in homosexual offers from the shadows. To top it off on the last day it looked like the hotel manager had cheated everyone with their bills. A few people had the temerity to complain but when they did three large, angry men immediately removed their luggage from the bus and only replaced it once they'd coughed up.

Instead of the relaxed sporting beach vacation I planned, I received a stupid package vacation I never wanted, all because they'd overbooked. Thank you, the world's favourite airline.

GRAHAM TAYLOR

'IT TURNED OUT TO BE A LOCAL CRUISING SPOT'

WELCOME PLEASE! FEEL FREE TO TREAT THE LAND OF OUR ANCESTORS LIKE A FUCKING SHIT HOLE

GWYH

REVOLTING LOCALS · Club Med recently attempted to build a 700-capacity vacation village in Kakome Bay, Albania. After loud protests from local villagers who claimed to have documents dating back to the days of King Zog that proved they owned the land, rendering the development illegal, the government sent in 600 Special Forces troops to quell their demonstration. The local mayor's mother was quoted in the *Guardian*, 'Even the Germans didn't behave like that.' The Albanian government has been accused of giving carte blanche to tourist developers in an attempt to bolster their economy and help their case for joining the EU.

36 IOS, GREECE

STRESS	💩	💩	💩	💩	·
SICKNESS	💩	💩	💩	·	·
BOREDOM	💩	·	·	·	·
DANGER	💩	·	·	·	·
EXPLOITATION	·	·	·	·	·

Duration: 1 week
Cost: ⊖350

My dad loved walking more than anything else, so every year he would pack all eight members of the family into an old green Land-Rover and drive to Wales or Scotland, where we would spend a week trooping in a long line over endless boggy hills. From a young age I wished for something else, a vacation like other families had, one that involved sunshine and foreign climes. The foreign beach vacation became my holy grail. Eventually in my late teens I scraped together enough money to go island hopping with two friends in Greece. No more packed lunches, no more thick damp socks, no more poring over maps. I spent the weeks before thinking beautiful thoughts. They all ended with me having sex with an exotic Mediterranean beauty, someone who found the charms of a young man negotiating safe passage between his past, as a miserable Smiths fan, and his destiny, as an up-for-it raver, irresistible. We caught the boat from Athens straight to the island of Ios, which in the late eighties had a reputation as a wild party island. My two friends, Andy and Dom, were both violently sea-sick during the crossing. Happily it didn't stop us all from getting terrifically pissed. We arrived in Ios, found a cheap room, and decamped to the beach. At last I had arrived. We found an empty spot and I carefully spread out the towel I had taken from my parents' airing cupboard the night before. There was something wrong. It was the size of a hanky whilst everyone else's was the size of a double bed. I had never heard of 'beach' towels and now felt ridiculously out of place. Not only that, but I was having problems with the sun. It was just too bright. I didn't own any sunglasses and had to really squint to read my pretentious book (Henry Miller's *Tropic of Capricorn*). I had some suntan lotion but had gone for the lowest factor, as I didn't really know how it worked. It was translucent yellow and once smeared on my bony white frame looked like someone had taken an almighty piss all over me and then rolled me in the sand. Half an hour later three Scandinavian girls walked past. They were all topless. I tried not to get an immediate erection. The tallest of them had short dyed blonde hair, an angry little face and tits the size of zeppelins. She stared at us and started laughing. Soon her friends had joined in. Looking down I saw I was already badly sunburnt. Disheartened, I rolled up my tiny towel and headed to the bar. Soon Andy and Dom joined me. For the next twelve hours we roamed the streets of Ios trying to get laid. We didn't manage to talk to anyone bar a racist crane driver from Essex who memorably called Andy 'a quiet cunt'. Eventually we decided it was time to give up and head home. When we got there we discovered someone had broken in. Nothing had been stolen but perched on my bed was a nervous-looking chicken. He was taking a shit. As I stripped off the sheets and climbed onto the thin strip of foam that was pretending to be a mattress I felt deflated; clearly the beach vacation was not the Shangri-La I had hoped for. I shut my eyes and dreamt of Wales.

MATHEW CLAYTON

BALCONY WITH EVERY ROOM

35 SPANISH CRUISE

STRESS	💩	💩	•	•	•
SICKNESS	💩	💩	💩	•	•
BOREDOM	💩	💩	💩	•	•
DANGER	•	•	•	•	•
EXPLOITATION	•	•	•	•	•

Duration: 2 nights
Cost: $350

I took a boat from Portsmouth to Bilbao with my wife and parents, forgoing the sane option of flight so that my father could bring his car. The trip takes two nights and is described in the brochure as a mini-cruise. Hard-partying pensioners made up the bulk of the passengers. One old man waved four cartons of Embassy filter at me and declared he had 'three more of these trips left in me before I go'. It wasn't a cruise at all. It was an adventure in voluntary euthanasia through the admin-istration of large doses of duty free. By day we played Virtua Cop in the arcades and sat on the desolate deck; by night we drank unremittingly. The Joe Loss Orchestra played big-band versions of MOR ballads and 'In the Mood'. My enjoyment of their set was marred by a persistent clicking noise that I took to be a faulty vent but which turned out to be the arthritic knees of the trombone section struggling to their feet. Joe Loss is dead, of course, and even the memory of him has all but leaked from our culture. In the bar afterwards I asked the band how they felt about this, but with all that cheap gin inside me it came out as, 'How the hell has the Joe Loss Orchestra survived the loss of Joe?' We landed at Bilbao at an obscenely early hour and I had to drag my still-drunk wife down six decks to the car bay. My father was beside himself with rage at our tardiness; we fell into his car with only seconds before the ferry door opened. Can there be a worse crime for the lower-middle class male than holding up the disembarkation of a car ferry? Unfortunately the combination of the hot revving engines and her hangover proved too much for my wife, who—as soon as we hit traffic on the way into Bilbao—methodically and tidily threw up in each section of my dad's *Sunday Times*. If only the Style section had been more absorbent, the upholstery would have been spared.

MATTHEW DE ABAITUA

34 CANAL BOAT-ING, ENGLAND

STRESS	💩 💩 💩 💩 💩
SICKNESS	• • • • •
BOREDOM	💩 💩 💩 • •
DANGER	💩 💩 • • •
EXPLOITATION	• • • • •

Duration: 1 week
Cost: $525

The worst vacation my family and our two unlucky guests ever had was a week-long barge trip down the River Thames in 1982. It should have been lovely: an easy glide through a pretty part of southeast England over sunny summer days, with ginger pop picnics on the banks and dreams of Bohemian freedom on the deck. But it was a freaking disaster from beginning to end. Running a barge requires a practical temperament, and my parents are not practical people. My father ran the boat aground every day without fail. On one afternoon he managed to get a rope caught up in the rudder, and was forced to spend two hours diving underneath the boat in his nerdy oversized swimming trunks, announcing every return above surface with a fresh batch of waterlogged expletives. Mum managed to get quite a good nautical look going in a striped top and white trousers, but she made the extremely un-nautical error of pushing the boat away from the side of a jetty without holding onto anything—which meant that we could only watch in suppressed hilarity as she slowly, but inevitably, plopped into the Thames. We boys amused ourselves as best we could. My elder brother had an uncommunicative French exchange student with him who decided to get homesick about halfway through the vacation. He spent mealtimes poking food around the plate with his fork before bursting into tears and running off into his (shared) cabin. My friend Will and I spent most of the time on the roof of the barge, amusing ourselves by making spiders fight gladiatorial battles with woodlice or forcing ladybirds to walk the plank. Vicious torture of creatures even more helpless than us was a natural response to the situation. Come to think of it, the vacation must have been particularly bad for Will. He can't swim and he's terrified of water. There were brief snatches of happiness. One evening we found a small

'IT WAS A CRUEL SOCIAL EXPERIMENT'

Island in the middle of the river, unoccupied save for a few coots, and I remember wading in its shallow banks at sunset, thinking about how beautiful England could be. Throughout the week we met fellow barge travellers more adept at life on the river than ourselves, and they always seemed happy to get us out of our daily crises. But what I remember most was the endless arguments, mostly between my parents. It was like a cruel social experiment: take a previously contented middle-class nuclear family, stuff them into a tiny space imprisoned by water, and put them through a series of practical tasks they have no hope of being able to do. And make them pay for the privilege. It is said that experiences like this bring a family together. However, shortly after the vacation my mother wrote two books. *Unholy Matrimony: The Case Against Marriage* and *Do You Really Want Children?* My father took up an Indian spiritual philosophy in which the goal is to leave the physical body altogether and elevate oneself to the astral plane. And then they sent me off to boarding school in Hampshire. Oh yes—and they got divorced.

WILL HODGINSON

THE END OF THE LINE

33 INTERRAILING IN EUROPE

STRESS	💩	💩	💩	💩	·
SICKNESS	·	·	·	·	·
BOREDOM	💩	💩	·	·	·
DANGER	💩	💩	💩	·	·
EXPLOITATION	·	·	·	·	·

Duration: 4 weeks
Cost: $885

'You can buy a bottle of beer for 25 cents,' was the recommendation that did it. Up until that point I had never even heard of Prague but back in the early nineties it was a rather hip place to go. Dutifully my friend Zack and I spent $440 each on an interrail pass and set off on an adventure to the exotic-sounding Czech Republic.

I felt like the great travel writer Bruce Chatwin as we climbed on the ferry from Dover to Calais. We were real travellers. We were part of a noble breed of adventurers seeking the open road and wise people from foreign lands. I had imagined, with a somewhat smug smile, that on the ferry we would stand out from the schmucks on their 'package vacations'. This romantic image vanished completely on arrival at Calais train station. I began to feel like one of a herd as our entire train carriage became filled with carbon copies of us. From the brand-new matching twenty-litre rucksacks from Millets to our gleaming Thompson's European rail timetables. Still, we did have an adventure. The bar in Lyon station at midnight was interesting. A large insane Frenchman put 'Sex Machine' by James Brown on the video jukebox twelve times in a row and fiercely stared out anyone who ventured within touching distance of 'his' jukebox. He was taunting us all—the unrivalled king of his domain. Ten minutes later a racially tattooed man came up to me on the deserted platform and tried to bum a cigarette. I had just lit my last one and, being somewhat deficient in my knowledge of French, gestured to him with my now empty cigarette box and shook my head as meekly as I could. He grinned a terrifying smile, plucked the cigarette out of my mouth, taking the skin off my top lip, and walked off laughing. I was far too timid to complain and thanked my lucky stars I hadn't been knifed. Then, after doing nothing in Venice because it was all so expensive, we embarked on a thirteen-hour train journey to Prague. We boarded the train, and set about trying to find somewhere to sit. The door to every carriage slammed in our faces. Extended families and their livestock seemed to have appropriated the entire train, leaving Zack and me to sit on the damp floor by the toilet. We took it in turns to stretch our feet into the single cubicle, the rest of the time we had to try and sleep cross-legged. Still, we were young. This was true travelling. Suffering was part of the attraction. It was a story to tell back at home. And Prague would be worth it. 25 cents a beer! We would live like kings! It may have been 25 cents for a beer once, but not anymore. Not after Europe's teenage herds had started descending en masse. The only hostel we could afford was a fifteen-minute tram ride alongside the river. We shared a room with a large man with a shock of red hair. He was one of those traveller types who really, really needed to go home. He'd taken so many drugs just being in the same room as him was enough to give you 'the fear'. Still, punk was all the rage in Prague in the nineties, so we headed off into the city for a bar called 'The Bunker'. En route we went into a strip bar and after putting the equivalent of twenty dollars in coins into a turnstile we wandered round a maze of red corridors until we found ourselves outside as the fire door closed behind us, leaving us both ashamed and broke. Still, at least we had 'The Bunker'. We could tell people about that when we got home. An hour later, after being advised to down four consecutive absinthes by a barman, Zack and I were aimlessly wandering around the town until a taxi picked us up. The driver proceeded to drop us off nowhere near our hostel, leaving us to walk the final mile or so back along the river. Out of the gloom we could see a car's dipped headlights. Being out of our minds on the 'green fairy', we stumbled up to it to see what was going on. It was a police car. And the two male officers inside were energetically giving each other blowjobs on the backseat. We took this as our cue to leave and legged it back in the direction of our hostel.

We only stopped off once in Amsterdam on the way home. We stayed in a room at the 'Twin Pigs Café' along with twelve other people. It stank. It was hot; we couldn't afford to buy a bottle of water. I urged Zack to take it in turns with me to stay up to keep an eye on our no-doubt murderous 'companions'. He refused so I stayed awake all night, peering out into the rancid darkness, imagining all kinds of horrors that would befall us. On our penultimate night on the 'Damrak' (Amsterdam's notorious high street) we got mugged. I was so relieved. At last we had a story we could terrify our parents with. Then we reboarded the ferry and limped home. When I got back I immediately and enthusiastically unfolded my map on the lounge floor to show my dad the route of our adventure. He got within three feet of me, smiled, turned round and said, 'Why don't I run you a bath?'

I'd be lying if I said it wasn't great fun. So why was it a crap vacation? Because it was like being stuck in a student union bar for three weeks. The other thing that was crap about it was the price. After we got home Zack and I calculated that, after spending in total $885 each, a two-week package vacation to Barbados would've been cheaper. **DOUG**

PHOTOGRAPH BY ANDREW DRUMMOND

THE HUMAN ZOO · The 'long necked' women of Burma's Padaung tribe have been a favourite curiosity for western tourists for some time. So much so that businessmen from Phuket in Thailand recently approached the tribe with a business proposition to buy five families to display to tourists. The local governor stepped in and the proposition was declined. The Padaung are used to such treatment however; a few years ago thirty-three of them were kidnapped and imprisoned in a fake village for eighteen months and forced to pose for tourist photographs.

32 IBIZA, SPAIN

STRESS	💩	💩	💩	💩	·	
SICKNESS	·	·	·	·	·	
BOREDOM	💩	💩	💩	·	·	
DANGER	💩	💩	💩	💩	💩	
EXPLOITATION	💩	💩	·	·	·	

Duration: 1 week
Cost: €440

People rave about the place, but let's get Ibiza into perspective immediately. My vacation there was so shit that I ended up as a refugee in a German vacation camp.

Four of us, a mixture of students and derelicts, had saved enough money through the summer to consider a last-minute holiday. It was Wednesday night in the pub when we first discussed the possibility, and by Saturday morning we were on a plane to the Balearics—a self-catering villa in Ibiza having been the cheapest cancellation we could find. I should have seen

the signs early on. The airplane seats were lined with 'Club 18–30' pissheads. The stewardesses looked terrified. And we were still only ten minutes from Gatwick. And then, a few hours later, there were 300 drunken Brits rolling around the arrival lounge in Ibiza Town airport, hurling abuse at baggage handlers, porters—in fact, anyone with olive skin. The famous British art of queuing was nonexistent as people actually fought each other in the taxi rank. We had to run across a dual carriageway pursued by a screaming peroxide blonde, in order to secure a cab, and, of course, the destination turned out to be a disaster. Our 'Luxury Villa' was part of a half-built block of flats on a building site, there was no one to let us in, and because it was three in the morning the nearest bar was shut. Surely things couldn't get any worse? I was glad of the black-label vodka. It maintained our sanity levels until 9 a.m., when someone turned up with some keys.

Settled in, we felt better and ventured off to cash our traveller's cheques. 'Where are you staying?' the rather abrupt woman behind the counter demanded. We told her. 'Then you can go elsewhere to cash your cheques—the guy who owns your block is a wanker.' 'So where is the nearest other place?' 'I'm not telling you, not when you're giving money to that bastard.' 'Right...' We searched in vain for an alternative Exchange Bureau but found nothing. I went back alone, and seriously begged, and begged and begged. They thankfully relented and I got some pesetas. The first bar was full of Englishmen fighting, much like the second, the third and the fourth. The fifth contained more Spaniards and with it a less volatile atmosphere. Jenz and I made ourselves comfortable at the bar while the girls strutted their stuff on the dance floor. Suddenly there was shrieking, and I turned to see some greasy local with a monster mullet manhandling my girlfriend. In fairness to him, my girlfriend was the biggest flirt in the world, but I was pissed and he was out of order. As he grabbed at her tits a red mist descended and suddenly I found myself running, then he was falling—right across the speaker stack. A huge bang was followed by brief silence and then a growling noise as I became surrounded by a group of fuming Spaniards. It was time to leave. The next place was also simmering with testosterone. I was feeling ashamed of myself, but was also angry with my girlfriend, who was once again dancing dirty in front of a slobbering audience. The mood was darkening as the club closed. A couple of scuffles had already occurred in the shadows, and I was desperate to get back to the flat. As we left, however, two of my girlfriend's latest admirers approached. 'Come on then, girl—let's go and fuck,' the first one snarled. In hindsight, a pretty bold opening gambit. I tried to keep cool. 'Sorry, lads, she's with me.' Within seconds things went mad. I was on the floor, my girlfriend was getting slapped, and some guy stood over me screaming, 'We're gonna murder you and rape your fucking girlfriend.' Meantime his mate had run to the boot of his car and produced a bullwhip, which he cracked in my direction—like Indiana Jones on angel dust. 'Oh shit,' I murmured. Then the cavalry arrived. Two cars screeched around the corner and the occupants poured out, waving baseball bats and making straight for Indiana and his mates. I didn't hang about to see the outcome.

As we approached home we stopped at a little taverna for a cold beer. We told the bargirl about our evening. 'That's the English end of town,' she said. 'It's the same every night. This, though, is the quiet German end. You should stay here.' So we did, she was right and our vacation was saved. **KEV**

'NOISE, ALCOHOL AND VOMIT'

31 DAYTONA BEACH, FLORIDA

STRESS	💩	💩	·	·	·
SICKNESS	💩	·	·	·	·
BOREDOM	💩	💩	·	·	·
DANGER	💩	💩	·	·	·
EXPLOITATION	💩	💩	💩	💩	·

Duration: N/A
Cost: N/A

After dropping out of university, I had the displeasure of living in the vacation resort of Daytona Beach, Florida, for five years.

The tourists who come to visit seem to love the place. Somehow, they manage not to see the hordes of homeless people sleeping rough anywhere they can find and crapping wherever they feel the urge. The spring-breakers who descend every year spew noise, alcohol and vomit all over the town. The work is all low-wage tourism work in fast-food joints and hotels. If you want a proper job, you have to commute an hour to Orlando, and even then, you are most likely to end up working at any one of a number of theme parks or resorts. And that's if you can get to your job in the first place. The bus system outside the tourist routes is crap; you can't possibly expect to arrive anywhere on time, even if you allow an extra hour. And as for buying a house, forget it. The housing costs, as a result of vacation homes, are outrageous, and impossible to afford on minimum wage. The landlords all want to cater to the tourists, and imagine themselves as 'vacation home' entrepreneurs. And then there are the hurricanes. Making minimum wage, you can't afford to get out of town and go inland during hurricane season. You board up your windows and sit it out. You can't even watch television, as the power is the first thing to go, quickly followed by the water.

This is one town that needs bombing off the face of the earth. **BETH**

30 KUTA, INDONESIA

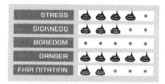

STRESS	💩	💩	💩	•	
SICKNESS	💩	💩	💩	•	
BOREDOM	•	•	•	•	•
DANGER	💩	💩	💩	💩	💩
EXPLOITATION	💩	💩	•	•	•

Duration: 8 weeks
Cost: $2650

I was trudging back along the dark streets of Kuta in Indonesia, midway through an eight-week tour of Asia, when I fell into a roadside storm drain affectionately known by the tourists as 'the Malaysian Mantrap'. It was no more than a foot and a half deep but I still managed to break my kneecap. I'm not a hard man, but sometimes the shock of an incident like that can do funny things to a person. I walked back to my hotel and up three flights of stairs to my crappy room. The pain was overwhelming to say the least by the time I got to my bed. It came in thick waves like acoustic thuds reverberating through my bones. And then the fever hit. It was fever coupled with extreme nausea. I was soaked in cold sweat, my head was dizzy and I began to

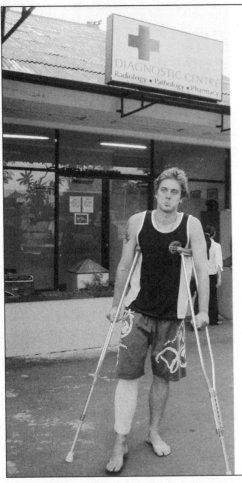

realize that things were far more serious than I had first presumed. I lay there for almost twenty-four hours, without painkillers or water but most importantly without a phone.

Eventually I managed to get hold of a friend in Bali who took me to a clinic just outside of Denpasar. My relief was tempered somewhat by my 'pal' photographing every agonizing stage of my medical procedures. Laughing hysterically, he shoved a camera in my face whilst a nurse stuck a hypodermic needle into my arm. What a pal. And for those of you who haven't had the pleasure of similar experiences, health insurance companies do not provide money for the cost of treatment up front. You have to cough up for whatever treatment needs to take place and then the companies reimburse you later. Penniless from losing my bag a week prior to my accident (after a bender in Singapore) my now not so plucky photographer pal was stuck with my medical bill. This may have been satisfying from my point of view, but it resulted in me receiving the cheapest, most ramshackle technology the hospital had to offer. I ended up with what had to be described as a 'third-world splint' on my leg, which my 'friend' spent twenty minutes trying to convince the staff he should do himself to keep the labour costs down. Then came the subject of crutches. He soon worked out that it could be more economical to actually purchase a pair rather than rent them, so I was soon given the most decrepit and outdated pair of injure sticks on the island. Now I'm no dedicated follower of contemporary crutch fashion, but these things were just unfair. They were the kind that go all the way up to your armpits, 'Dickensian' is the only word I can think of that gives any indication of just how old and grimy these things were. I limped back to my 'chateau de filth', looking like a crippled child from *Oliver Twist* and I tried not to think too much about what the future had in store. I was told that surgery was a big likelihood and that Indonesia would not be the best place to undergo such treatment. I spent a further week in my room, sustaining myself on a calcium-packed diet of biscuits and crisps, I read a lot through that time, and thought about my options as well as allowing my mind to ponder some of the more abstract possibilities. It

seemed that bad luck had surreptitiously attached itself to me somewhere along the crossing of Malaysia. I spent a while trying to recollect any old gypsy women I might have run over, or any witch doctors I might still owe money to. With either parent on equatorial opposites of the planet, it was only six days after the incident that they even found out. My father got on the phone and set about verbally chastising me, somehow making the sole topic of the phone call the electricity and phone bills I had left unpaid at home. Needless to say this wasn't the reception I'd been hoping for. Fortunately, I didn't need any actual help because I was insured. HSBC, BUPA and AMEX insurance pooled together to be precise. (Yes, I really am insured by three companies, owing to the fact that this was the third time I'd snapped my skeleton while abroad. I am now categorized as 'High Risk'.) I had my business-class flight to London organized within a couple of days. The option of undergoing the surgery in Singapore was there, but I would have incurred a massive expenditure just hanging about waiting for physiotherapy at outpatients, something my policies fail to cover, so I was homeward bound. On my last night, I checked into one of the most expensive hotels in Bali and called the in-house doctor to see what last load of sedatives and painkillers I could extract from the liberal hands of the Asian health care system. That evening he arrived, a short, podgy Indonesian fellow in his late fifties. Armed with a suitcase full of drugs, he was by far the most eccentric doctor I have ever met. As he commenced his 'consultation' by prancing around the hotel room on my crutches, it became apparent that this guy would give me anything I asked for, well, whatever he hadn't already finished off himself that afternoon. Not only did he present me with Valium for my incredibly flimsy 'I'm nervous about my leg' excuse, but he also provided me with sleeping pills so strong I felt tired just looking at them. 'You take these on plane...' he started, pointing to the Valium,

'you no scared no more......weeeee,' he said as he made a motion with his hand of a plane taking off. 'You have big smile.' He gestured to the sleeping pills. 'You take one of these....you no smile no more, my man, you sleeping eight hours, boosh...' He yawned as he slumped dramatically on the side of my bed. I enquired about the effects of alcohol with the drugs he was about to give me. He laughed maniacally. 'You crazy man....once I sleep a day after drink with these things...' Well, there's nothing like a bit of first-hand knowledge, is there? I bid him farewell, wondering if an unsuccessful career on stage had led him into the medical profession. What a guy. I wish he lived in England. As you can imagine I don't remember much about how I got home, I have a vague memory of being wheeled around Bali airport but now find myself safely ensconced on my dad's sofa. My brush with the Indonesian health system hasn't put me off the country, though. In fact I'm already planning a return trip. Providing I can get insured.

ELLIOT PURCHASE

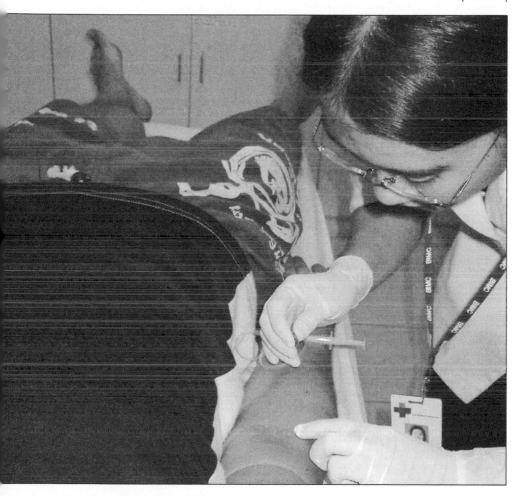

29 MONACO

STRESS	💩	💩	💩	💩	💩
SICKNESS	•	•	•	•	•
BOREDOM	•	•	•	•	•
DANGER	💩	💩	•	•	•
EXPLOITATION	•	•	•	•	•

Duration: 5 days
Cost: ₡710

In 1996 I tried to mix business with pleasure. I had arranged to interview the then current World Series of Poker champion, Huck Seed, in Monaco, for *GQ* magazine. We were to meet him at the World Backgammon Championships where he was competing. The few days travelling either side of the interview would be the nearest thing I'd had to a vacation in five years. I borrowed a friend's car and convinced a photographer pal, Adam, and my boyfriend, Hugo, to come along. I was on the dole, and paying for gas, road tolls and everyone's accommodation for the entire trip.

We stopped for a night in Dijon, which was silent after 7 p.m. except for the occasional scream. I gritted my teeth as I paid for the terrifying hotel. I knew I had gone over my overdraft limit but reasoned that it would ultimately be fine because the *GQ* fee and expenses would more than cover my costs.

The next day we arrived in St Raphael, in the south of France, with a glamorous journalistic commission and a few days' vacation on the French Riviera ahead. This was the life of my dreams. I'd found a free house for us to stay in, fifty miles east of Monaco, through a friend. In Monaco the World Backgammon Championships launch party was a grand champagne and

caviar do in a plush hotel suite that overhung the sea. Being from *GQ*, we were very popular. Princess somebody or other—a Russian with her face stretched—was wearing golden couture. She lavished me with attention. I was wearing a posh canary-yellow suit myself so I stood next to her, absorbing the idea that all this glitz was the perfect setting for my interview with Huck. Who, come to think of it, I hadn't yet spotted. I later learned from a drawling Texan that he had rescheduled and would now arrive the following day. Which meant another 100-mile return trip from the house. Shit.

The next day Huck didn't show up at all. I called and called but I couldn't get hold of him. The drawling Texan shrugged his shoulders when, on the verge of tears, I pestered him for answers. It turned out that Huck had decided not to bother coming after all. So there would be no interview. Bang went the *GQ* fee and expenses, bang went Adam's photography fee, and bang went my new image.

I was desperately upset and had the growing, icy realization that I was now also bankrupt. Hugo moaned about everything, especially my driving, and we had rows in the car, with Adam stuck in the back cringing with embarrassment. When we eventually got home I went to return the car to its owner. We had put over 2,000 miles on it, diminishing its value, and the week after I returned it, it broke down. I wriggled out of any financial responsibility, at the same time realizing that this was the kind of thing friends don't forget.

KIRA

'OUR SKIN PEELED OFF IN KEBAB-LIKE CHUNKS'

28 ISRAEL AND EGYPT

STRESS	💩💩💩💩 ·	
SICKNESS	💩💩💩💩💩	
BOREDOM	· · · · ·	
DANGER	💩💩💩💩 ·	
EXPLOITATION	· · · · ·	

Duration: 10 days
Cost: $795

Foolishly keen to sample the aquatic delights of diving in Egypt and the health-giving properties of Israel's Dead Sea, my two friends and I packed our trunks and headed out to Stansted airport, where our crap vacation began. Anyone who's ventured near an 'El Al' check-in desk will know that the procedures used by their employees can feel like the verbal equivalent of being slapped across the face. This savage parley went on for about forty-five minutes. They couldn't seem to fathom why three blokes would go to Israel 'on vacation'. Four hours after the barbarous introduction and a gin-and-tonic-saturated flight, we touched down in Tel Aviv to more people prodding us with rifles and asking us more tricky questions. After smoking a bit of pot with expat kibbutz escapees and attempting to charm the military girls of Tel Aviv, we lost no time in driving in dodgy rent-a-car with Israeli number plates right into Jericho in the mistaken belief that we were on our way to the Dead Sea. Owing to certain political forces, driving an Israeli car around there is like having a fucking great billboard permanently suspended above your head with the words 'Please attack' stencilled in metre-high lettering. After numerous pedestrian shouts, which roughly translated as 'I kill you!' and Arab residents hurling large rocks (I kid you not), we made it in the end to the Dead Sea, where we floated for the next three hours. We then realized that the maximum time one should spend in the Dead Sea is under forty-five minutes. This resulted in our extremely dry skin peeling off in kebab-like chunks in the mid-July sun.

Driving our frazzled hides to the border of Egypt, we deposited the rental car and trundled over the border to find more people wielding guns. Taking a taxi that looked like it was constructed from several deceased vans, exschool-trip coaches and an Austin Maestro, we arrived in Dahab. We then booked into a hotel—

or at least part of a hotel. Its hallway tapered off to a sheer drop. The shower had electric cables poking tendril-like out of the wall, which added to the excitement of being doused in lukewarm seawater. I promptly developed chronic diarrhoea by midafternoon. So bad were the anal emissions that I had to stay in the baking hotel room for the next two days. My only entertainment involved scorching passing cockroaches with my lighter and a can of deodorant. As for hooking up with a passing traveller, this was somewhat hindered when I lost my remaining contact lenses, which resulted in being able neither to see nor dive. The latter may not sound too much of a hindrance, but when one is competing to gain the affections of female travellers against hardened divers who bleat on about wrestling a ten-foot sea snake to the ocean floor, then it's a problem. I stayed marooned in the beach-side cafés staring into the middle distance, occasionally breaking wind and constantly being 'playfully' hassled by fifteen pre-pubescent Bedouin girls, goading me to buy bracelets and to gamble on games of backgammon, which inevitably ended in me losing a large quantity of shekels and having my sunglasses pinched.

The highlight had to be some show-off 'diver' desperately trying to impress some girls in the neighbouring room by climbing a palm tree (which, I might add, simply ran right through the three floors of the hotel). He immediately got stuck on the upward facing layers of spiky bark. After much laughter and prodding we realized the prongs of bark had actually pierced his clothes and skin and thus it took us fifteen minutes to disengage the hapless moron.

WILL HOGAN

ALL WORK AND NO PLAY

CRAP VACATION TRIVIA

American workers talk about vacations, plan for them, dream about them, and then never take them. According to a poll conducted for Expedia.com by Harris Interactive, Americans are likely to give back more than 421 million vacation days in 2005. Given a five-day workweek, that comes out to more than 1.6 million years of unused vacation.

27 STAYING AT HOME

STRESS	💩	💩	💩	💩	•
SICKNESS	•	•	•	•	•
BOREDOM	💩	💩	💩	💩	•
DANGER	•	•	•	•	•
EXPLOITATION	•	•	•	•	•

Duration: 2 weeks
Cost: Nothing

I had wangled two weeks for myself, in between changing jobs, where I planned to sit at home very, very still and do very, very little whilst stewing in my own filth, growing fat and drunk and developing an inordinately large thumb from obsessive and manic channel surfing. But I managed only two days of 'nothing', and not even a proper nothing at that.

As soon as folk get wind of you having time off and the fact that you're planning to do nothing with it, they get ideas in their head about helping you to occupy your time. Grandmothers imagine that you would be much edified by cutting their grass, digging their garden, running their errands and generally attending to the detritus that has gathered for generations in their sheds, garages, huts, alcoves, porches, closets and attics. Aunts and cousins (the lady type) decide their offspring could benefit from the company of 'a man about the place', the neglected little mites never having known their own fathers; such is the modus operandi of the modern paterfamilias. So I played football, crawled around the garden on all fours (the grass having just been neatly cut) with bloated cherubs astride my back, threw infant after infant into the air (a queue formed around my block of the abandoned offspring of the track-suit-wearing, feathery moustachioed inbreds and halfwits of the locality). My parents then reminded me of the lifetime of sacrifice they devoted to me and started calling in the debt. So I was sequestered into making trips to the local dump after spending a weekend cutting trees, grass and gathering junk, etc.

It was exhausting. Now I understand why my friends go on package vacations.

BARRIE CREAMER

26 SWEDISH EXCHANGE

STRESS	💩	💩	💩	💩	·
SICKNESS	·	·	·	·	·
BOREDOM	💩	💩	·	·	·
DANGER	💩	💩	💩	💩	·
EXPLOITATION	·	·	·	·	·

Duration: 7 days
Cost. ¢825

Our headmaster had twinned my close-knit parochial primary with a school in a small town in Sweden. My pen pal turned out to be Johan and we had exchanged letters for a year before I made the trip over the North Sea, with my class, to meet in Scandinavia Johan, from his picture, filled the Aryan stereotype of a Swede to a T. Blond hair and blue eyes complete with small, molish golden-framed spectacles. This was my first trip away without my mum and dad. I disembarked, already homesick, and a Volvo coach took us to the school to meet our cousins from the continent. When we met, the first thing I noticed was that Johan was tall—excessively tall, being almost double my height. His mother led me into the house (gripping my hand as though I were prey that might escape). It was very late, and so we two eleven-year-olds were sent straight to bed and the lights were switched off.

My bed wasn't quite as comfortable as Johan's looked. Essentially they had just thrown a sleeping bag on the wooden floor. 'Godnaat,' his mother said before ominously locking the door behind her. Exhausted and in my pyjamas by now, I began to drift off to sleep until I was awoken by the sound of Johan's computer being switched on. His Amiga spluttered to life and he inserted a blue disk. It fired up and suddenly crudely animated hardcore porn dominated the screen. The imagery was so badly rendered that one had to squint to make out who was licking or jiggery-poking who—or what for that matter. Johan was now wide-eyed and kept turning to me asking 'Like it?' as a blond Scandinavian licked a pixilated bell end. 'Like it? Like it?' I nodded feebly. He stayed glued to the screen until the early hours, watching it on a loop.

When the morning came I was led into the bathroom to wash, a bath already having been run for me. There was no lock on the door (why not in here but a lock on the bedroom door?)

HOME SWEDE HOME

and I lay in the tub terrified that someone would walk in. Johan's mother did, five times. I resorted to shyly cupping my balls every time she entered to check I was ok.

I was at the table by 7.30 a.m., where ham and cheese made for an agreeable breakfast. Agreeable that is until Johan's father entered the room. He was naked except for the kind of Y-fronts that protect genital modesty but display a mesh of pubes, filtered through white cotton, his obese belly drooping over those wholly inadequate underpants. I gagged. He went to the fridge, grinning and asked his family repeatedly, whilst pointing at me, 'English?' 'Ja!' they all replied— Mum, Johan and his imaginatively named little sister, Johanna. 'English?' 'Ja!' Despite the early hour he pulled a beer out of the fridge and sat next to me. His flabby buttocks sank over the edge of his seat and gripped the kitchen chair. He looked directly at me, scraped the blond fringe from his eyes and asked:

'English?' 'Ja?' I replied, hoping this was the right answer. 'YES!' he screamed, and the whole family joined in. He cracked his can open and took a long swig. 'YES, YES! HA HA! YES!' I looked at my watch to check the date. Oh God. It would be one whole week before I would be on the plane home. In those seven days I spent half of my time enjoyably with my classmates on field trips. The other half was spent in this Swedish homestead with the Jo twins, the hand-squeezing mad-mum and the obese alcoholic father. To this day, despite the beautiful lakes and the altogether charming town, my abiding memory of Sweden is the sound of a deathly white, fat and flabby drunken man with a hairy back, laughing insanely at a television in his sweaty pants, as I lie cowering in a tepid bath, covering as best I can my prepubescent balls.

LIAM

CRAP VACATION TRIVIA

THE WORST VACATION ON EARTH?

Pauline Arnold and her friend Ruth Oliphant booked a spur-of-the-moment luxury vacation to the Dominican Republic through Thomas Cook in February 2005. But things didn't turn out quite as they'd hoped. Within days of arrival both Pauline and Ruth had contracted severe diarrhoea. Then the hotel's water system backed up, leaving their overflowing toilet bowl unflushable. Pauline was quoted in the *Bedfordshire on Sunday* newspaper: 'The stench was absolutely appalling. It was bad enough having chronic diarrhoea, but then not being able to flush the toilet was totally unbearable.' The catalogue of catastrophic events continued. Both ladies were forced to visit the emergency doctor four times during their trip, where they found other hacked-off tourists, standing in corridors, hooked up with intravenous drips. Finally, on the day they were due to fly home a catering truck crashed into their plane, causing their flight to be cancelled. When they did finally get on a plane to Heathrow the following day, they discovered that instead of flying direct, as they had been told, they would be stopping off to refuel. In Canada. Thomas Cook apologized and urged other unsatisfied customers to contact their customer service team.

25 SWINDON, ENGLAND

STRESS	💩	💩	•	•	•
SICKNESS	💩	•	•	•	•
BOREDOM	💩	💩	💩	💩	💩
DANGER	💩	💩	💩	•	•
EXPLOITATION	•	•	•	•	•

Duration: 16 hours
Cost: $160

It's probably my own fault. As a man with stock phrases, using 'like a wet weekend in Swindon' as the last word in pejoratives for any dreary event was probably asking for trouble. But then the year before, my girlfriend had taken us to Rome for my birthday, so you could understand why I got excited when just before the next birthday she'd told me to leave the weekend clear and pack a bag. She didn't explicitly mention a passport, but I packed it anyway. I guess she didn't really know what she was letting us in for. After all, she was from Birmingham.

We lasted less than twenty-four hours. From the dingy hotel with its hysterical guide to the highpoints and history of Swindon (including the claim that the band Oasis had taken their name from the town's leisure center) to an afternoon at some particularly rancid retail park on the other side of town, it was just a protracted trudge through a grimy seventies theme park. We still held out hopes for the evening's entertainment, although when the least vile bar we could find was some kind of confused Che Guevara kitsch job we should have known it was a non-starter. I can't remember where we ate—I suspect that's not because it was unmemorable but because it was so unspeakably bad I've battled long and hard to keep it deeply buried in the closet of my mind—but I do remember the chilling moment when we realized that the best the evening offered was a Specials covers band at the pub near our hotel. We stuck it out in the upstairs bar, just able to make out the sound of 'Too Much Too Young' being murdered through the floorboards until we gave up and headed back to the hotel. We would have made our own entertainment, but ten hours in Swindon could dampen Colin Farrell's libido. We left by 9 a.m. virtually running to the station. I've never been so pleased to see West London.

LEE FISHER

24 DUBROVNIK, YUGOSLAVIA

STRESS	•	•	•	•	•
SICKNESS	•	•	•	•	•
BOREDOM	•	•	•	•	•
DANGER	💩	💩	💩	💩	💩
EXPLOITATION	💩	💩	💩	💩	💩

Duration: 2 weeks
Cost: ₤1400

Before it was bombed back to the Stone Age in the nineties, Yugoslavia was quite the destination for the adventurous holidaymaker, my parents being amongst them, and so it was that in the summer of 1976 the four-year-old version of myself was excitedly sat within the confines of a Boeing 707 headed for Dubrovnik for our first family vacation abroad. No complaints about this 'pearl of the Balkans' with its azure coastline, friendly citizens, fine food and numerous Volkswagen Beetles (strange what you remember as a boy). Indeed my father's passion and natural talent for photography has allowed me to look over happy photographs from that very fortnight for many years. It wasn't until a few years ago that my father, perhaps having gorged on especially strong rum & raisin ice-cream, told me something rather sinister had occurred on my first trip abroad. Apparently it happened over lunch one day whilst eating some glorious seafood dish by the port, that a friendly local man started chatting to my parents about the area, sites of interest and what have you. After sharing a drink or two with him and doubtless becoming comfortable with his Yugoslavian charms, they then freely agreed to his request that he 'borrow the boy' for a short time. Off I trotted with this stranger, hand-in-hand, whilst they continued to chow down on the kind of cuisine that was the stuff of a Captain Bluebeard fisherman's tale. After about twenty-five minutes, according to my father, they both started to wonder where I might have been taken, and what indeed this jovial gent might actually be doing with me. Doubtless they soon realized that they wouldn't have let some hairy Yugoslavian male take me from their care in the Grimsby Riverhead Shopping Centre, yet here they were having freely handed their only child to what could have easily been the Balkan town's very own Jeffrey Dahmer. It was just at that moment that I reappeared, alone and, as

'I REAPPEARED, ALONE AND DRUNK AS A LORD'

my father humourlessly put it, 'as drunk as a Lord'. I sought to confirm this story with my mother, who upon being regaled with the facts simply turned bright red and claimed 'not to know what he was talking about'. So, there's my first family vacation for you—consisting as it did of the sweet-and-sour juxtaposition of seeing a beautiful city prior to its complete and utter ruin with my young untarnished eyes, and narrowly avoiding being sold to a pre-Internet paedophile ring having been plied with fruity alcohol and perhaps fiddled with in some rather unsavoury manner. Thankfully I don't remember any of this, and as you are printing my name would like to point out that I remain sexually well adjusted.
PAUL VINTER

23 PARIS, FRANCE

STRESS	
SICKNESS	
BOREDOM	
DANGER	
EXPLOITATION	

Duration: N/A
Cost: N/A

Parisians are legendarily arrogant and rude, which is surprising when you think that nothing of any great value has come from the city in a hundred fucking years. They whine and they mince around wearing stupid glasses and ridiculously collared shirts. They're totally irrelevant in every area of modern life except in the utterly pointless charade that is the world of fashion. I mean I know I'm generalizing a trifle here, but imagine a country historically characterized by its cowardice, hypocrisy and cruel food strutting around the world's stage with its nose in the air? Paris is beautiful though, not that any of its current residents can take any credit for that.

RIK

France is the most popular international vacation destination on earth, with 77 million arrivals a year. That's equal to the total international tourist arrivals of the US (41.9 million), UK (24.2 million) and Thailand (10.9 million) combined.

22 SLAPTON SANDS, ENGLAND

STRESS		
SICKNESS		
BOREDOM		
DANGER		
EXPLOITATION		

Duration: 2 weeks
Cost: $140

Our family suffered a few financial setbacks that lasted for the entire 1970s. In fact, matters didn't improve much until my parents divorced shortly after our vacation on Slapton Sands. Of course, destitution and marital anomie have never stood in the way of that great British tradition, the truly miserable annual excursion; in fact, they are essential.

The summer of 1977 failed to live up to 1976's scorching glory. Being a few years shy of puberty, and not quite ready to pogo with the punks, I'd suffered the Silver Jubilee along with the rest of Her Majesty's loyal subjects. My biggest act of rebellion was to drink the jubilee pale ale, which my father bought me as a souvenir—advising me to hang on to it, as it would eventually be valuable. This is all beside the point of course—which I am now coming to. Two weeks in a caravan in a field on a farm in Slapton Sands in Devon. One small hedge away from a pigsty, no mod cons, hot water sporadically available from the farmhouse up the hill across the mud-slicked farmyard, and several miles from the beach. This was probably not mentioned in the small ad in the *Exchange and Mart* that caught Dad's eye. It was, as he pointed out in answer to all complaints, cheap, and when he was a boy, his only vacation was spent at a TB sanatorium. In retrospect, of course, fair play to him. At least we weren't cordoned off from the rest of society.

The beach of Slapton Sands is, as its name suggests, a sandy beach. Very similar to France, my dad said. What he failed to mention was that

SUN, SEA AND LAND MINES

it had been used to rehearse for the D-Day landings, with live ammunition and land mines, many of which were still there. This is of course a matter of public record now, but back then, it was still under the official secrets act fifty-year rule—as was the fact that as many men died here as in the actual battle. There wasn't much sun, though, as far as I remember.

There were not many holidaymakers on the beach, which these days would be a plus, but back then just added to our sense of isolation. Old men with metal detectors and warm clothing wished us good afternoon and continued along the beach. Not all their machines had the headphone facility, and those who had were so deaf that they needed full volume.

The ambient sounds of those endless summer days would have given *The Wire* magazine a collective orgasm, but to us it was just eerie and threatening. The police and army turned up twice to evacuate the beach when these old boys found live mines. Danger Unexploded Bomb signs were put up, which had been stored in a beach hut—obviously in situ due to frequent use. It can't be many family vacations where you leave the beach by retracing the footprints you made while coming on to it.

As I mentioned before, I had not quite embraced punk rock, and fully intended to go rockabilly as soon as I was old enough to rock 'n' roll. The news that Elvis Presley had cancelled all future engagements on the earth was the icing on the cake.

Having moaned so much about these two weeks out of the many thousand I have survived seems a little churlish now. Especially as they stick so vividly in my mind. I am glad my dad was my dad and didn't take us to Spain or Majorca or Butlins. No he said, it was cheap.

JOHN MOORE

21 CLUB 18–30, KAVOS, GREECE

STRESS	🌀 🌀 🌀 · ·
SICKNESS	🌀 🌀 🌀 🌀 🌀
BOREDOM	· · · · ·
DANGER	🌀 🌀 🌀 🌀 🌀
EXPLOITATION	🌀 🌀 · · ·

Duration: 1 week
Cost: $425

You've got to try it once. Well, no you haven't, but I did. The vacation was a bit tedious to be honest, but I did discover something that most visitors to these types of resorts don't read about in the brochures. The locals are always moaning about English people puking in the streets, and the local police have no time for English people puking in the streets, but why is it that so many English people puke in the streets? I'm sure 90% of them do because they have no self-control, but some of it has to be blamed on the local liquor, which isn't quite what it seems. I'd been in the town with my

GWYN

mates for three hours. We'd had a few shots and a couple of pints but nothing too heavy. I began to feel a gut-wrenching pain in my stomach that was swiftly followed by a fountain of vomit. After half an hour all six of us had chucked up. Feeling somewhat sheepish, and putting it down to the flight, heat, etc, we shrugged it off and went to find a club. Later on, our guts still somewhat bewildered, we started talking to one of the reps, who was trying to get us to go into the club she worked for. The subject of our puking came up, in conversation, so to speak. She smiled. 'Stick to the bottled beer. Never, whatever you do, drink the spirits in any of the bars on the strip. The barmen top them up with meths. I'm, not joking. They fucking hate you English.'

JACK

20 MOUNT SINAI, EGYPT

STRESS	💩 💩 💩 💩 💩
SICKNESS	• • • • •
BOREDOM	💩 💩 💩 💩 •
DANGER	💩 💩 💩 • •
EXPLOITATION	• • • • •

Duration: 1 week
Cost: Nothing

A couple of years ago I started seeing a new girlfriend (whom I shall call M), who only five weeks into the relationship suggested we went away on vacation together. Despite my misgivings that it was a bit soon for such things, she insisted that she had a good 'two for the price of one' deal, and that I may as well go. So I went. The trip was to the Red Sea, and I didn't have to pay for anything; a week of free food, beer, sun, sea and sex...it sounded great. Unfortunately, M turned out to be a whinging, paranoid, jealous, desperate weirdo who stuck to me like a limpet. If I so much as looked in the general direction of any woman wearing a bikini (hard not to do on a beach) I got a tearful earful about being an ungrateful, lecherous bastard. I was her prisoner. In desperation, for a bit of freedom and fun, I opted into everything going, all the water-sports, the diving, the trekking, seeking anything that I

THE 'KAVOS COUGH'

CRAP VACATION TRIVIA

Holidaymakers are being overcharged for nonexistent illnesses according to research carried out by the BBC. One tourist went to a local doctor complaining of a nasty cold only to be told that she had contracted a mysterious ailment and would need to spend a night in hospital. After her insurance details were taken she was whisked off. Locals confirmed the 'Kavos cough' was a well-known health insurance scam that has been going on in Greece for over twenty years.

thought she'd turn down with a weary, 'No, you go, I'll just lie by the pool'. No such luck.

The high and low points came on one of the excursions offered; a trek up Mount Sinai (where Moses received the Ten Commandments). The idea was you climbed it at night so as to watch the sun rise from the top. It sounded fantastic. This involved a couple of hours' coach journey through the desert, a camel trek, and a three-hour climb, after leaving the hotel at 11 p.m. All of this sounded like it might just be too much effort for M, so I jumped at the chance. Alas, she insisted on coming too. Unfortunately, she neglected to mention that she suffered from both night-blindness and vertigo, so perhaps climbing a mountain in the dark wasn't the best idea.

'SHE SUFFERED FROM VERTIGO AND NIGHT-BLINDNESS'

Things began to go wrong on the coach. We picked up another party from a nearby hotel, amongst whom was a very friendly and pretty girl who insisted on talking to us. Any attempt at a response to her conversation from me was met with an elbow in the ribs. When we finally arrived at the drop-off we hiked to the camel-station where noisy Bedouins tried to encourage us

to get on their camels. It was a confusion of darkness and torches, campfires, roaring and charging camels and about 150 tourists in several parties, and we quickly got separated from our group. As soon as I mounted my camel, the guide rushed us away as he wanted to join a party that was just leaving for the trek up the lower slopes. I looked around in vain for M, but couldn't see her, so assumed that she was on the camel behind and that she would catch us up at one of the many stopping points. Despite the initial chaos, the actual trek up the mountain was one of the most magical events of my life, and I heartily recommend it to anyone: the swaying camels, the darkness, the cries of the Bedouins, the millions of stars... Best of all, I was free, if only for a short while. Eventually, another camel, occupied by the pretty girl from the coach, lolloped along next to me. We chatted, and started to get on rather well. Eventually, we reached the point where the camels could go no further, and we alighted, ready to continue the last part of the journey on foot. We decided to sit down and wait for the rest of our party and continued to chat. Over an hour later, M stumbled into view, blinking like a mole and being led by a middle-aged German, at precisely the moment when the pretty girl was giving me her e-mail address. M was incandescent with rage, and I had to wait a good half hour before I could even begin to get a word in. It transpired that when her camel reared up to its full height, M's vertigo had kicked in and she had had to get off, leaving her alone and in the dark (I had the only torch). She'd had to make her way up the mountain, on foot, was exhausted, bruised, bitter, humiliated and furious. It was only her fear of being left behind that led her to make the arduous uphill climb. We did eventually make it to the top, and watched the sun rise in silence, for which I was thankful, as it would have spoiled the sheer beauty of it to have her whining continue. But if the trip up the mountain was bad, the trip back down again was even worse. Now that dawn had broken it meant that M could see the steepness of the mountain we had to climb down. Her vertigo kicked in again, which meant she got dizzy on virtually every rock more than an inch high and had to be coaxed and cajoled to take even the smallest step. To make matters worse the pretty girl stayed with us, chatting gaily and leaping from rock to rock with the grace of a gazelle, which must have annoyed M even more. I needn't go on. The relationship did not survive the holiday. We parted at Gatwick airport (where she called me a sponging freeloader!) and I never saw her again. Thank God.

ROBERT

19 KLOSTERS, SWITZERLAND

STRESS	💩	💩	💩	💩	💩
SICKNESS	•	•	•	•	•
BOREDOM	💩	💩	💩	💩	•
DANGER	💩	💩	💩	💩	💩
EXPLOITATION	•	•	•	•	•

Duration: 2 weeks
Cost: $790

It's probably unfair to label the ski resort of Klosters as a crap vacation destination seeing as I never actually made it anywhere near the slopes but it is by far the worst vacation I've ever had. Things started going awry at the airport, when a couple of tossers with public school haircuts started dissing me for having a snowboard. They all sniggered at me in the departure lounge before one of them shouted, 'Gays on Trays,' while looking up innocently at the air above my head. This had them all reeling around in hysterics as I sat stunned and bewildered by their utter twatishness.

It was, nonetheless, a bad omen that had me on edge for the entire flight. I don't like to think that it affected my balance on the stairs as I disembarked from the plane (it would make a painful memory even more depressing) but something odd definitely happened. I can't

crunch on the tarmac at the bottom. My right arm broke somehow on the way down and my left gave way as I crashed into the ground. The concussion I managed to pick up from several of the steps on the way down. This story may sound apocryphal, but I can assure you that these wounds have taken years to heal. After I came to my senses in hospital, my bowels threatened to open as I remembered that I hadn't taken out holiday insurance. I sat, panic stricken, with a head twice its normal size, praying there'd been no need for a helicopter to bring me to the hospital. And then, just when I thought things couldn't possibly get any worse, a nurse resembling giant haystacks came over and saw my no doubt terrified expression. She smiled calmly at me, shook her head and said in a strange accent, 'Don't worry, I vipe your bottom.'

RIK

explain what exactly because I suffered extreme concussion and woke up in a hospital bed with a bandage around my head and both of my arms in plaster. I imagined at the time that it would all come back to me at some point, but it hasn't happened yet. It appears that my fellow travellers thought I was dead after I fell down the entire flight of steps and landed with a

THE FIVE MOST DANGEROUS VACATIONS ON EARTH

Most of us go on vacation to relax, put our feet up and have a well-deserved rest. But, bizarrely, for some vacations are a chance to push themselves against the elements and flirt with death...

5 KAKADU NATIONAL PARK, AUSTRALIA

Sea crocodile numbers in Kakadu National Park have risen dramatically in the last few years, and consequently certain parts of the park have been closed to the public.

However, tour operators have met the possibility of tourists being eaten alive with skepticism. One reportedly said, 'A lot of us have questioned the existence of crocodiles in that area, but maybe they really are there.' This opinion is surprising. Only two years ago a German backpacker was dragged to her death by a crocodile after going for a midnight swim in one of the park's swimming holes.

4 MOUNTAIN-BIKING THE YUNGAS ROAD IN BOLIVIA

The Yungas road has claimed the lives of many since it was completed in 1935 with an astonishing 200 people dying in one year alone. For most people that would make it the last road you would ever want to travel. That is unless you're an adrenaline junkie mountain-biker, in which case it's the ideal vacation destination. A thirty-eight-mile journey swooping down from the Andean mountains into the Amazon rainforest sounds wonderful, but the reality is a treacherous winding road lined with flowers and shrines to the thousands of people who have perished while driving along it. There are no safety barriers along the route, in places there is only enough room for traffic to pass in single file and the nearest hospital is over two hours away. According to one traveller, 'The slightest lapse in concentration will send you to toppling to your death.'

③ FIRST CONTACT, PAPUA ADVENTURES, INDONESIA

One of the few places where anthropologists believe it is still possible to find civilizations that remain untouched by the modern world is in West Papua, Indonesia. Papua Adventures, run by Kelly Woolford, offer three-week 'First Contact' vacations there in what they call 'full-on exploratory expeditions'.

However, seeking out undiscovered tribes hundreds of miles from civilization can be a dangerous business. One tourist, a journalist working for *Outside* magazine, reported stumbling across a death adder (one of the deadliest snakes in Papua), being chased by screaming natives and then having to swim across a crocodile-infested river to escape flying arrows. But the authenticity of Woolford's expeditions has been called into question by leading anthropologists, one of whom declared, 'I'm 95 percent sure it's a hoax.'

Woolford refutes these accusations and suggests that anyone who doesn't believe his tours are authentic should go with him into the jungle and experience it for themselves. Papua Adventures ($7,400 per person for a 21-day trek)

② OPERATION SHILOH, ISRAEL

Operation Shiloh is an Israeli anti-terrorist vacation camp. Set up by Yehoshua Mizrachi and Jay Greenwald in the aftermath of the terrorist attacks of 9/11, Operation Shiloh uses Special Forces troops to teach civilians military tactics. One of the terror tourists, Lisa Reed, told the BBC, 'Primarily I want to know what I can do to protect myself and my family from a terrorist attack on my neighbourhood.' Operation Shiloh includes training in how to use Uzi machine guns and hand-to-hand combat. Once the tourists have perfected these skills, they take on Israeli troops pretending to be Arab terrorists. After that they go on their final excursion—a patrol around one of the most dangerous cities on earth, Hebron in Palestine, under military curfew. The Palestinian Authority has condemned the program. Operation Shiloh ($5,500 per person); www.opshiloh.com

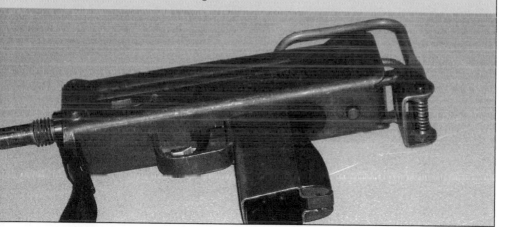

1 CLIMBING MOUNT EVEREST

Perhaps not the most obvious vacation destination, Mount Everest is, however, becoming increasingly popular with tourists seeking an extreme adventure. K2 is widely considered to be the most difficult mountain in the world to climb, but Everest is the most dangerous. The plethora of dangers facing climbers include avalanches, wind speeds of up to 120 mph, changing weather conditions, storms, temperatures of minus 40 degrees Fahrenheit and oxygen deprivation. Above 25,000 feet you will find yourself in the 'death zone', where oxygen levels are two-thirds lower than at sea level. Here you will be more likely to succumb to hypothermia, frostbite, high-altitude pulmonary edema (where your lungs fill with fluid and you drown) and high-altitude cerebral edema (where your oxygen-starved brain swells up). Even if you take bottled oxygen, you'll experience extreme fatigue, impaired judgement and coordination, headaches, nausea, double vision and hallucinations.

Everest is littered with bodies. If you decide to attempt the climb, you have a one in six chance of not coming back down again, and if you do find yourself getting into trouble don't think you'll be able to rely on your fellow climbers to help you get back down. As one experienced climber put it, 'There's no such thing as morality above 25,000 ft.'

18 SCHOOL CRUISE

STRESS	💩💩💩💩 •
SICKNESS	💩💩 • • •
BOREDOM	💩💩💩💩💩
DANGER	💩💩💩 • •
EXPLOITATION	💩💩💩 • •

Duration: 10 days
Cost: $990

When I was at school I went on a cruise to Egypt, Israel, Turkey and Greece. For anyone thinking this was some posh school and some luxury trip, let me stop you right there. This was a no-frills pack-'em-in, out-of-season torture fest. The week before we went, the boat we were due to go on sank off the coast of Italy. Bedraggled school kids were airlifted to safety and the company's 'reserve' liner was brought into action for our cruise.

It must have been an ex-

EXPERIENCE THE BREATHTAKING
BEAUTY OF THE NILE

prison liner. Our cabin was so low in the depths of the boat that it took ten minutes to walk down all the stairs. In the light of the previous boat's difficulties, safety was one of the more pressing issues on our minds. There were no fire extinguishers, none of us had any idea how to get out if we had to and kids just ran wild down the corridors. On-the-spot beatings were issued from each school's bullies, while the teachers reclined and got pissed in the more luxurious cabins at the top of the boat. Mealtimes consisted of a long walk down into the dark corners of the boat to the kitchens, where you were issued with a metal tray filled with ladles of unknown slop from pissed-off-looking Africans. The gruel was so bad I lived off bread rolls for the entire week. When we finally got to Egypt, after an inevitably puke-filled voyage, we got on a bus for a three-hour drive to see the pyramids. The company had arranged packed lunches, which they had stowed in the racks above our seats. Jeremy Guild pulled his box down and disturbed a large community of cockroaches that rained down on top of him.

After regaining our composure we arrived at Giza. Everyone had been warned about the dubious nature of the characters that preyed on young tourists and we were specifically told not to accept the offer of camel rides. We all took heed of this advice. Everyone that is except for Chloe Richards, who was taken out into the middle of the desert on a camel and relieved of all her money and possessions. She eventually made her way back to the coach, screaming her head off. Mr Bunting went off in a rage to 'kick the crap out of the fucking wog bastard'.

On one night my nerdy friends and I attempted to keep a low profile and escape the attentions of the various bullies who prowled the corridors by hiding in our cabin. Sadly for us our very own bully, Gordon Bruce, was determined to find his regular punch-bags. However, luckily for me my good but undeniably stupid friend Michael had decided to strip down to his pants and wrap himself in Saran wrap (he was always rather odd), which Gordon was happy to rip off him before shaving my head and my friend Glen's eyebrows. He then took a shower with Diane in the cabin opposite (whom I was secretly in love with) before spending the night loudly shagging her senseless.

Next stop Israel, the Wailing Wall and the Dead Sea. Chloe Richards was still in a state of distress after her previous ordeal and refused to get off the coach when she saw the machine guns being held by the prowling soldiers at the Wailing Wall. Later, when we went for a swim, I broke my glasses getting changed, while Gordon attempted to drown Michael in the Dead Sea. Last stop Turkey, where it seemed everyone was determined to buy a cheap leather jacket. After hours of searching the bazaar Michael finally bought one and rolled his shoulders smugly all the way back to the ship. Then Gordon pointed out that the zip was on the right side not the left, which, according to him, meant Michael had bought 'a bird's jacket'. Cue much laughter from everyone while Michael, fighting back the tears, buried his new purchase into his bag. I decided to treat myself and spent the last of my meagre spending money on a bootleg copy of Bon Jovi's album *New Jersey* from a stall at Athens airport. I switched on my Walkman when I sat down on the plane only for the mechanism to immediately chew up the tape. And just when things couldn't get any worse, Gordon sat behind me and proceeded to spend the entire four-hour flight kicking the back of my seat. The bastard.

This sad story does have a happy ending though. I just looked up Gordon on Friends Reunited and today he passes the time selling turnips door-to-door. Us nerds, meanwhile, have inherited the earth.

K.K.

GERMANS JUST WANT TO HAVE FUN · According to a Berlin travel agency, Germans work so hard that they've forgotten how to enjoy themselves. In an attempt to restore a healthy work/life balance, the agency has organized a training course to teach workaholic parents how to build sandcastles and play with their children. They have been inundated with bookings.

17 GUERNSEY, CHANNEL ISLANDS

STRESS	💩💩💩💩 ·
SICKNESS	💩💩💩 · ·
BOREDOM	· · · · ·
DANGER	💩💩💩💩 ·
EXPLOITATION	· · · · ·

Duration: 1 week
Cost: £920

Nestled within shouting distance of France, but mercifully still within the boundaries of the UK, Guernsey is a quaint little island usually overshadowed by its larger neighbour Jersey. My brother moved there and regaled me with stories of its languid and peaceful charm. He said that the worst thing ever mentioned on the news was when someone lost their cat. After a particularly harrowing few months working for the Red Cross in Sarajevo, a week in June on a restful, slumbering island that was only an hour from Southampton airport was just what I'd been looking for.

I had been there for three peaceful days, and things were going fine until the particularly eventful fourth day. We ventured to a beach on the far western side of the island by bus. As we stepped off it a car mowed down a small child running across the road right in front of me. Thankfully he survived, but only just. The ambulance driver said he was lucky only to have broken both his legs. Absentmindedly, I then neglected to put sun cream on either of my feet. This resulted in agonizing, blistering sunburn on both of them for the rest of my stay. Later that night, after I'd calmed down and drenched my stinging feet with after-sun, I hobbled towards a bar with my brother. As we approached the door a bouncer made thunderous noises before throwing a drunk down some stone steps, causing the man to break his skull on the pavement right by my sore, blistered feet. He began bleeding profusely over my shoes. The air became filled with the metallic stench of blood that will be familiar to anyone who's worked in Casualty or a war-zone. It was precisely the kind of thing I'd gone on vacation to avoid. The flashbacks of gunfire and screaming mangled bodies on

DANGER ISLAND

stretchers came thick and fast. After vainly attompting to stem the flow of blood, while being careful not to move the poor man's head, the all too familiar ambulance arrived. The paramedic looked at me in surprise but assured me that if they got to the hospital without delay the man would be fine. I promptly threw up and staggered, gibbering, back up the road, my already frayed nerves stretched to the limit. My brother assures me that it was an aberration, but to me Guernsey is filed in my brain as one of the most dangerous places on earth.

GAZ

'THE MOTEL HAD NO POOL, DESPITE HAVING A SIGN THAT SAID IT DID'

16 RAPID CITY, SOUTH DAKOTA

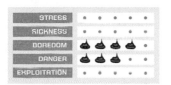

STRESS	•	•	•	•	•
SICKNESS	•	•	•	•	•
BOREDOM	💩	💩	💩	💩	•
DANGER	💩	💩	•	•	•
EXPLOITATION	•	•	•	•	•

Duration: 2 days
Cost: $265

You get to Rapid City, South Dakota, on a combination of Greyhound buses and foolish hopes. I had time to kill before I needed to be on the West Coast and pointless landmarks have always been things I have loved, so the king of them all, Mount Rushmore, was something I felt I had to see with my own eyes before they stopped working.

The motel I was booked in had no pool, despite having a sign that said they did. They offered me the use of a pool in a motel up the road, but it was hosting a convention of creepy crawlies. It was so hot I went in anyway. I got badly bitten.

The next day I took a tour coach out to Mount Rushmore, and learnt six and a half interesting facts about its construction, its history and its sculptor, Gutzon Borglum. The placing of an artificial landmark by a roadside in a landscape otherwise beautiful for its bleakness is a great American tradition, one we have imported half-heartedly. The trouble with all these objects is that while you might want to stand in the foreground of a photo of them, they have no other purpose. Mount Rushmore was faraway up a hill of shavings, and it didn't even look that big. I had come to South Dakota to look at something from a closer distance than I would if I'd stayed further away. If you'll excuse the pun, it put too much fucking perspective on things.

In the evening there was little to do in Rapid City. After looking at some great big dinosaurs you could actually get close to—proven by the vandalized brontosaurus—I went to the only cinema in town. It was showing *Batman and Robin*, which I had seen already, but even though I'd regretted even seeing it once it was kind of appropriate that I came all the way to Rapid City, South Dakota, to regret seeing it for the second time.

REUBEN MORGAN

15 PALOLEM, GOA, INDIA

STRESS	💩 💩 💩 💩 ·
SICKNESS	💩 💩 💩 💩 💩
BOREDOM	💩 · · · ·
DANGER	💩 💩 💩 · ·
EXPLOITATION	💩 💩 💩 · ·

Duration: 3 weeks
Cost: $875

After arriving in the idyllic beach of Palolem in Goa, I settled into a charming beach hut, where I planned to spend the rest of my well-earned vacation reading and taking yoga classes. I spent the day sunbathing and chatting to the extraordinarily friendly local men. For dinner I had one of the best curries of my life, washed down with a sweet lassi. I had been invited to a rooftop party, but as I was still jet-lagged, I said goodbye to my new pals and made my way back to the hut. I woke up at midnight with a faint rumbling in my stomach. Within ten minutes, the rumbling had become gurgling, and the gurgling had become gut-wrenching agony. I legged it into the 'bathroom' but just failed to reach the rancid hole in the ground that served as my toilet. I was so relieved that the pain had subsided, I hardly cared that both my legs and the floor had been sprayed with shit. I did my best to clear up the mess, whilst planning my secret escape from the hotel the next morning. I fell into bed feeling like a proper hardcore traveller and was just drifting off to sleep when the awful gurgling returned. This time I made it to the hole, squatted down, braced myself for another bout of squitters, only for the rest of my delicious curry to exit rapidly from my throat. After several more exhausting trips from bed to bathroom, I gave up and collapsed on the floor, miserable and sweating. I remained there for the rest of the night, interrupted every ten minutes by stinking water and mucus simultaneously shooting out of both ends. Next morning, weak and dehydrated, I gathered myself together for a desperately needed shower. After several minutes of wrestling with an apparently broken showerhead, I was salivating over the prospect of cleaning away the stench. I turned the knob, put my head back and was treated to a splatter of raw sewage. Palolem is supposed to have the most beautiful sunsets on the subcontinent, but

I didn't see a single one. My *Lonely Planet* diagnosed me with dysentery, and I remained in a similar state for the rest of my time there. You wouldn't think my vacation could get any worse, but just before I came home, I managed to get conned out of $350 by some phoney gem merchants. I arrived home skinny and broke.

AMELIA SAGE

14 LOS ANGELES, CALIFORNIA

STRESS	💩 💩 💩 💩 •
SICKNESS	• • • • •
BOREDOM	• • • • •
DANGER	💩 💩 💩 💩 💩
EXPLOITATION	• • • • •

Duration: 2 weeks
Cost: $2125

'Got a gun in your glove compartment?' the burly security man wheezed. 'Er, no,' came my defensive reply. 'Well, get one,' he grunted. That, it seems, is the standard tourist welcome at LA's rent-a-car lobby. Inspired by this initial excitement, my girlfriend, best mate and I then purchased a map from a man with absurdly flared nostrils (each about the size of a small doughnut) and set off on our two-week road trip of America. We then tentatively rolled out of the car park. The coffee–charged

residents of LA encouraged us on our way by scaring the living shit out of us, honking, cussing and generally saying 'get out the Goddamn way'—in various dialects and tones. Trying to ask for directions simply led to accusations of being from another planet, 'for real' or Australian.

We went from being considerably lost to considerably shafted. A sign for Compton loomed and passed. Compton? I mused. Hadn't I heard this name before? Of course—NWA's album—*Straight Outta Compton*! Compton effectively resembles a large life-sized barbecue. Burnt-out cars, bikes, skateboards, children and dogs saluted our path. One crack-addled harpy suggested we 'get the fuck outta here, honky!' She then promptly made this a lot more difficult by planting her obese, bulbous arse cheek right on the bonnet of our car and insisting we give her $10 to tell to us the right way. We did. We left. At that time, with my youthful, 'Martin Kemp' of Spandau Ballet fame style hair, in the sweet heat of July, I discovered that my cheap green hair-gel clearly wasn't designed to handle such searing temperatures. So much so that my fore-head became a luminescent shade of opal. This proved a source of great hilarity and consternation for my travelling companions and those we encountered through Death Valley on our way to Malibu and Nevada. Death Valley is so called for a reason. People die there, often. It's hot. So hot, it's like having thirty-eight hairdryers blowing on you from every possible direction. The signs on the side of the road tell you to turn your air conditioning off and on again intermittently every 25 miles. The reason soon became apparent. The car overheated and plumes of smoke and steam cascaded from the gaps in the bonnet. There's also a fallacy that when this happens you simply 'pop the hood', drink a coke and pull on your Levi 501s. When my navigator popped said hood the scorching steam seared her cheeks and scalded her nose. After much crying and water-pouring we got the car going again and went on our way. The roads to and from Death Valley also house some of the most in-bred hicks on the planet. I didn't think teeth were classed as luxury items until a few furtive enquiries in motels and diners proved otherwise. A visit to the local newsagent's revealed a high-quality publication on the front rack bearing the legend *Guns and Cunts*, which highlighted the interests of the local populace. Then it was on to Vegas. If you mix three British idiots with the remainder of their vacation money, a few martinis and a roulette wheel, you get the obvious result. Needless to say our holiday was cut shorter than anticipated and the staple diet for the remainder of our time revolved around Taco Bell meal deals and Holiday Inn breakfasts. Burnt, green-headed and broke, we left.

WILL HOGAN

13 SALTCOATS, SCOTLAND

STRESS	💩	💩	💩	💩	·
SICKNESS	💩	💩	·	·	·
BOREDOM	💩	💩	💩	💩	💩
DANGER	💩	💩	💩	💩	💩
EXPLOITATION	·	·	·	·	·

Duration: 1 week
Cost: $160

The ugliest place to go on vacation in the UK is a small seaside town called Saltcoats in Scotland. It has a caravan park that's nestled between an abattoir, full of distressed baying cows awaiting slaughter, and a chemical chimney, spewing sulphurous smoke over bottom-of-the-range static caravans. Walk into town in the morning and you'll pass the creatures all lined up ready for the slaughter and then, on your return from the bustling cosmopolitan metropolis that is Saltcoats, you can view the bones being conveyed into a large bin at the other end of the factory. Throw in an overexposed beach where one can view the manoeuvres of Britain's nuclear submarine fleet without binoculars and a bunch of locals sitting in sheds selling whelks in vinegar on the pier down the road and you start to get the picture. The final insult is the weather. The relentless, battering rain colours everything –the sky, the air, the ground and the buildings. Consequently the entire place morphs into a melancholic shade of suicidal rainwater grey.

HEATHER

12 BUCHAREST, ROMANIA

STRESS		
SICKNESS		
BOREDOM		
DANGER		
EXPLOITATION		

Duration: 10 days
Cost: $840

Everything that you imagine is true. Corrupt state-run dictatorships are no fun, especially if you are twelve years old. We began in Bucharest. A large department store, perhaps once a grand emporium of delights in pre-Communist Romania, that had the most disturbing window display I have ever seen. It consisted of two dusty grey sneakers on a concrete slab. Now of course if you saw that today, in some trendy Soho shop window, you might—assuming you are a pretentious tosser—enjoy its witty minimalist deconstruction of fashion, consumption and physical identity codes. But when you see grey battered sneakers, with the implication that this is the best this big capital-city store has to offer, it presents only the stuff of nightmares for those of us ingrained with the consumerist urges. The TV was poor. Yet it was still TV so I watched it. There was only one channel. A glum-faced man introduced endless clips of Ceaușescu visiting factories filled with forced-smile proletarians. Occasionally this was interspersed by violently disturbing abstract examples of Eastern European animation, scary enough to give the sneakers a run for their money.

The seaside resort itself had been built in a brutal Stalinist style that made London's South Bank look like a Taj Mahal of romantic expressionism. I boldly declared my bourgeois individuality by boycotting the yucky dinner and existed entirely on dry biscuits and pale lemonade. All the hotel guests, apart from myself, contracted botulism within five days of our arrival. For the first time in history, a fussy eater had been blessed by the rarely immanent patron saint of the overly picky, St Solopoulet. So I felt good about that, at least.

It was tough to be a holiday rep, waiter or concierge in Romania in 1970. At the time, Romanian law expressly forbade any conversation with foreigners. The smallest request

LIFT & PEEL HERE

QUALITY CONTROL
Blurred out of focus prints
*Focussing error - hold camera steady
*Camera shake - applies to variable focus cameras
*Subject too close - allow 2 metre distance for fixed focus cameras
*Dirt or condensation on lens
ADVICE LABEL

directed at a barman or waiter would therefore be greeted by an initial expression of fear, followed quickly by bitter resentment, topped up with a deathly acquiescence to fate. Staff turnover at the vacation resort must have been high. At the end of our vacation the tour rep, hotel manager and various waiters all suddenly vanished. A quiet, tremulous new hotel manager informed us that they had all been arrested for crimes relating to discourse with foreigners. The new guy knew that he too was living on borrowed time. Believe me, Kafka couldn't have made it up.

Those days are gone now of course. But should you ever wish to experience a similarly nightmarish kaleidoscope of Kafkaesque proportions I suggest that you attempt to ask for a full refund for a nonfunctioning item purchased from any electrical emporium on the high street.

GREG ROWLAND

11 AFANDOU, GREECE

STRESS	💩	💩	💩	·	·
SICKNESS	💩	💩	💩	·	·
BOREDOM	💩	💩	💩	·	·
DANGER	💩	·	·	·	·
EXPLOITATION	·	·	·	·	·

Duration: 2 weeks
Cost: $495

A few years ago when I was nineteen, my mate Chris began a never-ending campaign of persuasion to convince me to go on holiday to Greece with his girlfriend and three of her mates. I figured I would pretend to be eager to go with them and when the actual time to book arrived I would plead poverty. 'That's shite, Neil, now you've left me to go on vacation with a bunch of annoying birds,' Chris said, forgetting that one of those 'birds' was actually his girlfriend. Well, my conscience got the better of me and I reluctantly phoned up the travel agent and got a single apartment in the small town near Greece's 'party capital' Faliraki, where Chris was staying with his gaggle of ladies. It was called Afandou. The nightmare began when I was dropped off at my apartment. Chris and 'friends' were in the main town and would be dropped after me. I fumbled down the dark pathway to my apartment and was not surprised to find that there wasn't a fan in my room. It was five o'clock in the morning, 95°F, and after five pints of lager at Manchester airport and two Jack and cokes on the plane I was somewhat dehydrated. The tour rep had cheerfully reminded me to avoid tap water because it was a 'bit iffy'. With this warning in mind and no shops in sight to buy water I began to understand what it must be like to find oneself in an Iranian jail. The frustration I had boiling a pot of tap water and waiting for it to cool whilst crying out for sleep was only topped the next day when I found out that Chris et al. had been dropped off outside a shop and spent an hour swimming in their moonlit pool as the sun rose before falling calmly asleep until the early afternoon.

After a few days we met Keith and Jonathan from Birmingham. I figured they were decent enough guys and we all headed into Faliraki one night. Not being into dancing that much, Chris and I sat at a table whilst Keith and Jonathan danced with the girls. Soon the girls started joining us at our table. 'It's disgusting, Keith has totally got a hard-on and he keeps rubbing it up against us,' said Alison. Soon all of the girls had retreated to our table in disgust, with the exception of one—Chris's girlfriend, Julie, who seemed to be having the time of her life. There should be a word for the emotion that encapsulates disgust, anger, jealousy and self-pity into one, because this was what Chris was experiencing. For the rest of the vacation Chris and Julie had blazing rows about this incident, leaving me in the company of four girls I had absolutely nothing in common with. I began to say things to them just to piss them off and have an argument about. Otherwise each night would have been spent in deathly silence. Chris's package included breakfast, but this didn't make the vacation any easier on him. Each morning he would be confronted by a sleazy Greek waiter who had absolutely no grasp of English or it seemed Greek for that matter, unless you had breasts and blond hair in which case he spoke English like a BBC news-reader.

I agreed to come in for Chris on our last night so we could go out for one last crap adventure. At 9 o'clock I walked up the street to his apart-ment. A crying Julie ran past me, shouting something about 'that bastard'. I walked up to find Chris's door slightly open. I found him on the end of his bed staring blankly into space, pick-ing up coat hangers from a pile and snapping them before throwing the pieces onto a pile on the floor. He only had to say 'Just leave' once before I slowly backed out the door. To top it all off, on the very last day, I realized that I had been the unsuspecting victim of a seventy-year-old voyeur. Having spent every morning comatose in bed from the previous night's booz-ing I usually didn't wake up until around one. Complete nakedness was the only way to get a decent sleep. For some reason I hadn't noticed that the previous night's clothes would always be folded neatly on the spare bed beside mine. As I left a sun-wrinkled Greek lady with grey hair grinned slyly and said 'Hellooo' whilst star-ing at my crotch. She then entered my apart-ment and started busily preparing it for her next victims/guests.

NEIL WILSON

10 LAS VEGAS, NEVADA

STRESS	💩	💩	💩	·	·
SICKNESS	·	·	·	·	·
BOREDOM	·	·	·	·	·
DANGER	💩	💩	💩	·	·
EXPLOITATION	💩	💩	💩	💩	💩

Duration: 5 days
Cost: $1290.

Ah, Vegas. Never has a city been so enshrined with glamorous wrongdoing than Nevada's Vegas. Sharp suits, sunshine and Sinatra. I'd heard all the stories. Free drinks while you're betting, dancing girls and the insane bravado of the neon-drenched hotels. It was my turn to discover the glamour: my turn to spin the wheels that turned the cogs of the American Dream. Sadly the reality was somewhat at odds with my imagination.

Vacationing in Vegas is like being bludgeoned into a greed-induced coma, a coma punctuated with tawdry neon and the fat sausage-like fingers of the obese half-wits that fill its pointless slot arcades. Why not join the herds of these vacuous morons in tent-sized Hawaiian shirts, then you too can develop a 'Slot Hump' that even Quasimodo would find alarming? Then again, Vegas really is the centre of entertainment, if by entertainment you mean the relentless wailing of endless has-beens. Failing that, why not spend $70 watching the latest 'magical' performance from David Copperfield? Or perhaps you'd prefer to gouge out your own eyes with a complimentary hotel shoehorn? Then there are the casinos themselves. Holy Mother of Christ. Why not just join the tramps that are mercilessly hounded out of town and throw your hard-earned dollar bills into their trashcan fires to keep them warm? At least that way you'll be parted with your money but won't have to endure the constant whine of a million air-conditioning units almost single-handedly rocketing the earth into the clutches of global warming. 'But what about the half-size Eiffel Tower, the mock canals of Venice or the pyramids even? Surely Vegas is worth it for these spectacles alone!' Whoa there, no need to visit Paris then, Italy or one of the globe's earliest civilizations. While we're at it, fuck actually leaving the USA at all when you can see tacky reproductions of some of the world's most

breathtaking landmarks converted into tasteless hotels. Bugsy Segal had an epiphany crossing the Nevada desert. You can imagine his thought process. 'Why go through the hassle of stealing money from hard working people when you can get the morons to hand it over voluntarily in the name of "pleasure".' Hey, presto, Vegas was born.

RIK

09 BLACKPOOL, ENGLAND

STRESS	💩 💩 💩 · ·
SICKNESS	💩 💩 💩 💩 ·
BOREDOM	💩 💩 💩 💩 ·
DANGER	💩 💩 💩 · ·
EXPLOITATION	· · · · ·

Duration: 1 week
Cost: $160

This disgusting excuse for a vacation resort has gotten progressively worse since I first visited it in the 1970s. The only reason you need a bucket and spade in Blackpool is to scoop the dog crap and condoms off the sand before you sit down.

Quite how you can enjoy the 'great British vacation' in this cruddy resort is beyond me. Unless of course the great British vacation consists of drinking thirty pints of Carling, puking over everything that moves, punching anyone that comes within six feet of you, defecating in a bus shelter, and then catching some hideous disease from some ugly slapper on a coach trip from Grimsby.

DOUG WILLIAMSON

BRITAIN'S MOST POPULAR
HOLIDAY DESTINATION

08 CYPRUS AND EGYPT

STRESS	💩	💩	💩	💩	·
SICKNESS	💩	💩	💩	💩	💩
BOREDOM	💩	·	·	·	·
DANGER	💩	💩	💩	·	·
EXPLOITATION	·	·	·	·	·

Duration: 2 weeks
Cost: $3540

My first time abroad was a marvellous one in Cyprus. There was seasickness, food poisoning, a mini-golf fracas, and arguments aplenty—all to a comical Zorba-the-Greek style bouzouki soundtrack.

My brother Paul and I were glad of a break, the idea of swapping Croydon for Cyprus for a couple of weeks and a hit of sea and sunshine on the Isle of Athena was definitely preferable to our usual location—sandwiched between the sewage works and the landfill opposite IKEA.

So off we went with my ma and pa. To take you through the sensory experiences en route; ELO on the car stereo all the way to Gatwick; some sort of rank stew on the plane; a balmy black night; the drive through industrial Cypriot backwaters; the cold marble floor of our hotel; scratchy brown sheets; foreign-tasting water; foreign-smelling air; then time to wake up. I love that dark feeling of a curtained hotel room in a warm country. You draw back the curtains to beautiful sea and sand and blazing sunshine. One evening Paul was sitting down to a huge whole fish, and I had some sort of whole roasted baby lamb. Delighted with his menu choice, Paul pronged the milky eye of his fish and popped it in his mouth. We had a technique of ordering food that, put in simple terms, meant ordering the most expensive thing on the menu (and we still do it). No one could argue that ours was not a superb ordering technique, but neither of us enjoyed our meals very much. Afterwards we went out to 'Fantastico! Minigolf!' and some local youths took a disliking to my papa. Whilst regarding our game, they shouted insults to him from over the top of a fence. 'Hey, Mister, fuck you, hey, Mister, hey, Mister, yeah you, Mister. Go fuck yourself!' This went on for some considerable time until my dad, having gone quite red in the face, had to be restrained from kicking down a small wooden windmill and cracking each of the young

scamps in the temple with his golf club.

One day we decided to go to Egypt on a boat. The trip was dirt cheap, and like most young people I had always dreamt of going to Egypt. So I talked my parents into letting us all go. The next day we boarded the *Atalanté*, a less than splendid cruise ship covered in a patchwork of rust and ruin. The sea was 20 foot high and we rolled all day and night; my ma got quite green and uncommunicative, as did many of the other passengers. A constant trail of spew directed us up and down stairwells and corridors. The on-board entertainment was extraordinarily good. The main man was called Steve Zebs; he introduced himself on the microphone from behind a curtain, '...And now here is your host, Mr STEEEEEEVE Zebs!' He and his four dancing girls then proceeded to wow us all night with a medley of eighties classics and dance routines somewhat thwarted by the motion of the sea. The dancing girls fell all over the place and Steve Zebs split his imitation leather trousers during a rendition of 'Bad' by Michael Jackson. At the end of this spectacular show we were introduced

to our captain, 'Captain Dikeos Fokas!' My family literally fell apart and started crying with laughter and then someone was sick. It was the perfect end to the perfect day.

We arrived in Port Said for sunrise and it was beautiful. Breakfast in the dining room had to be enjoyed whilst wearing long trousers and so my pups endeavoured to find his only pair of 'chinos'. My mother had thoughtfully packed them next to his damp swimming trunks and now they had a blue and green nautical pattern on the seat area and Father was not best pleased. An enormous argument erupted in their cabin next door, and my brother went to investigate the hoo-ha. He soon ran back into our cabin to fill me in on the whys and wherefores of the ruined trousers and whose fault it was anyway, etc. Pa was still screeching and blathering through the thin wall and I, understandably, thought the situation was quite funny, so I laughed. Pops then pounded on the wall so hard I thought his fist would come through and I could practically see his raging red face, spittle gathering in the corners of his mouth, sweat beading out over his perplexed forehead as he screamed, 'I'm glad you think it's funny, you CUNT!' This only made me laugh more but quite scared the chambermaid, who was wheeling past at the time and decided to give us a miss tidying-wise. Mr Steve Zebs was also in charge of ladling the breakfast slop and handing out the two spam rolls and a banana (laid out in a rude way) that passed as lunch for our day trip to the land of the pharaohs. The breakfast slop was so incredibly poisonous looking that I couldn't touch it. It appeared to be spam chunks mixed with tinned vegetable salad. The edges were yellow and congealed and it was clearly inedible. My pops and brother managed to stomach a few mouthfuls, although later they did shit blood.

We drove for hours through the desert before we hit Cairo, then we had a whistle-stop tour of the Cairo museum, mummies, more mummies, Tutankhamun's mask, precious treasures and then back to the bus. Then on to the pyramids, pyramid, another pyramid; once you've seen one pyramid you've seen them all. We clambered back onto the bus. Drove through miles of desert, I saw a hoopoe, I saw the City of the Dead, lots of eagles, we got back onto the boat, back over the rolling waves and back to Cyprus.

SARAH JANES

CRAP VACATION TRIVIA

THE MOST EXPENSIVE HOTEL IN THE WORLD

For those with an appetite for real luxury, why not stay in the Burj Al Arab Hotel in Dubai? (The only seven-star hotel in the world.) Standing at 321 metres high, the hotel boasts: panoramic views of the Arabian Gulf, eight restaurants, a Rolls-Royce airport limousine service, two swimming pools, health spas, fitness studios, oriental massage, 42-inch plasma TVs in every room, exclusive full-size Hermès amenities (whatever they are), unlimited access to the Wild Wadi Water Park, and a personal butler for every room. A deluxe twin room, encompassing 335 square metres, costs a mind-blowing $3,600 per night.

07 BARBADOS, CARIBBEAN

STRESS					
SICKNESS					
ANHLUOM					
DANGER					
EXPLOITATION					

Duration: 2 weeks
Cost: $150,500

The worst vacation I ever had was all Tony Blackburn's fault. A hobby of mine used to be reading the autobiographies of Radio One disc jockeys, and I think it was while reading *The Living Legend* by Tony Blackburn that I came across a reference to a well-known posh hotel in Barbados. Blackburn described how he'd rubbed shoulders with some other celebrity on the beach there. As a teenager I'd sat listening to the radio every morning, wondering how you got from the dull, depressing world where I lived to the bright, sunny place where Tony Blackburn was. Now I knew the answer. Tony had shown me the way. I had to go to this well-known posh hotel in Barbados. It was many years before I could afford to make the journey. In the meantime I kept reading snippets about the hotel—apparently Cilla Black, Bob Monkhouse and Michael Winner were regulars. But this celebrity Shangri-La was still way beyond my reach.

By 1993 my situation had changed dramatically. *Viz* magazine, which I started, had been incredibly successful in the late 1980s, but despite considerable financial success my life was still pretty mundane. I didn't feel particularly rich or successful. The time had definitely come to visit Barbados, so I went to Newcastle's poshest travel agent and paid the price of a small house for a package vacation, which included first-class air fares to Barbados and a suite of rooms at the famed hotel for myself, my wife and our two young children. This was not only going to be the vacation of a lifetime, it was going to be a life-changing experience. I was going to pass through its mystic portal and into the sun-kissed celebrity lifestyle that lay beyond. It was my passage into the other world where Tony Blackburn lived. Alas, things didn't go according to plan. The hotel itself was OK, and the weather was probably great. I didn't really notice, as I spent much of the time locked in our bathroom desperately trying to avoid the attention of the hotel staff. The bastards waited on you hand and foot. Every door was opened for you, dining chairs pulled out for you—and then pushed in for you once you'd lowered your arse onto them. All the other posh guests were perfectly happy to gracefully bend their knees and lower their posteriors, trusting the waiter to put a chair in the right place at the right time. But I had to clutch the seat firmly with both hands before I committed my arse to that final descent. The waiters saw straight through me. That telltale grasping of the chair, the Marks & Spencer faux boating trip attire, and my uncultured choice of wine marked me out as an impostor. New money. At the poolside the drinks waiter could tell we weren't real guests. Instead of offering us drinks, he asked us if we'd go and do some duty-free shopping for him. He wanted a new pair of training shoes. While my wife, Dolores, was driven into town in the hotel's courtesy limousine, to get the waiter his new training shoes, I stayed by the pool with the kids. I briefly turned my back on the eldest, who was four, and just caught a glimpse of his head disappearing under the water as he toddled towards the deep end. In a panic I swam to him, pulled him up and carried him to the edge of the pool. His screams attracted a small crowd of disapproving onlookers who stood around tutting. I bought him some ice-cream to shut him up, and the crowd eventually dispersed. When my wife returned he told her all about how he'd drowned, and been given some ice-cream as a treat afterwards. Despite my heroic lifesaving dash I was in the bad books for several days. Tony Blackburn never showed up, nor did any of his show-business mates. The bar where I expected to relax and sip cocktails with Cilla Black was virtually a no-go area. Every bloke in the place looked like Enrique Iglesias. I looked like a sweaty Rush fucking Limbaugh. All around you over-attentive waiters lined the walls, like ball boys at Wimbledon, waiting to pounce. There was a bowl of nuts on the table, and every time I ate a nut a waiter would appear, whisk the bowl away, and replace it with a new one. If you tipped a cigarette in an ashtray it was immediately replaced. You didn't dare sip your drink in case they took that away as well. You were on tenterhooks. Sitting back in your chair and getting merry was out of the question. To get away from the intimidating atmosphere one evening we went on a sunset boat trip and sailed straight into the eye of a tropical storm. One of the crew hadn't turned up, so our small yacht was undermanned to begin with. We couldn't get into harbour for fear of being dashed on the rocks, so instead we had to sail out to sea. There, for ten or twenty minutes we just held onto the boat as hard as we could. It was like being on the Tilt-a-Whirl, with no seat belts, in the middle of the ocean. That trip just about summed up the vacation. I've never been happier to get home.

Saying it was the worst holiday I've ever had would be unfair to the hotel, which was, and still is, one of the world's best hotels. But as far as I'm concerned Tony Blackburn and his mates are welcome to it. It was a touch too sophisticated for me.

CHRIS DONALD

06 ORLANDO, FLORIDA

STRESS	💩 💩 💩 · ·
SICKNESS	💩 · · · ·
BOREDOM	💩 💩 💩 💩 ·
DANGER	💩 💩 💩 💩 💩
EXPLOITATION	💩 · · · ·

Duration: N/A
Cost: N/A

Picture the pointless blight that is Las Vegas, subtract the vice, add lots of humidity and flies, and then place the whole mess in a Wal-Mart parking lot...and apparently what you are left with is the place where people from American crap towns vacation. I dare anyone to locate a business that is not a chain, or a structure that is original, or a natural landmark of any kind. Life here takes place behind one enormous façade. The local population sequesters itself into a mundane patchwork of gated communities. There is actually a significant young population here, but they seem contented to live life in what are really glorified retirement communities. And I haven't even mentioned the wellspring of high culture that is Disney.

JOHN-PAUL CARDOSO

THE NEW OK CORRAL

Florida's tourists are being warned about the risk of Wild West–style shoot-outs in its city streets after new legislation was passed through the Florida senate in April 2005. Previously, if you were attacked in a public place the law demanded that you attempt to run away before resorting to violence. The new bill gives citizens the freedom to shoot dead anyone who threatens them in the street. Dennis Baxley, the Republican sponsor of the Stand Your Ground bill, commented, 'If I'm attacked, I should not have to retreat.'

CRAP VACATION TRIVIA

05 SAN SALVADOR, EL SALVADOR

STRESS	💩💩💩💩 ·	
SICKNESS	· · · · ·	
BOREDOM	💩💩 · · ·	
DANGER	💩💩💩💩💩	
EXPLOITATION	💩💩💩💩 ·	

Duration: 2 days
Cost: ₵320

I had five great weeks in Brazil almost ruined by two miserable days in San Salvador.

Day one: we jump off the bus at Salvador bus terminal and get straight into a taxi. Our friendly driver gives us a few pointers about what to see in the town, and what we should be wary of. He considerately warns us that as 'gringos' people will attempt to rip us off, before grossly overcharging us for the ride. After checking into our squalid hotel room, we decide to explore the historically distinguished, architecturally stunning ex-capital of Brazil. As we wander the streets, attempting not to get mugged at gunpoint becomes the least of our problems. Children cajole us from all directions, tying 'lucky' ribbons on our wrists and attempting to pickpocket us. We meet a trio of guys at a market stall. The first wears a long flowing traditional gown. The second attaches yet more ribbons on our wrists. The third tells us that he is a gangster who could break our necks if he felt like it, so we'd better watch out. He repeatedly asks us to flick his biceps for reasons never fully made clear. We make noises about having to be somewhere else. For a laugh, gangster man tells flowing gown man that our polite conversational laughter is actually more sinister and that we are actually taking the piss out of him for looking like a transvestite. As we leave, we are informed that we will meet these people again, at which point we will be injured quite badly.

We eventually do escape and decide to go for a quiet drink. Within minutes an almost entirely bald prostitute has planted herself in the seat next to us and is helping herself to our 'choppe' (beer). We tell her 'NO'. We tell her to 'GO AWAY'. We try to ignore her, but she has taken me for a potential client. She buys us a beer each, which we decide not to touch. She suddenly tries to kiss me. I recoil backwards into a large woman at another table. Without

'WITHIN MINUTES A BALD
PROSTITUTE SAT NEXT TO US'

warning, the prostitute then grabs my face and bites my nose. I'm utterly horrified. Realizing that she's not going to get a sale, she begins screaming at us, resulting in an entire street full of people staring at us. We sense danger, again, and get up to leave. The fat woman from the other table taps me on the shoulder. 'Argentino?' she asks me. 'Nao. Inglés.' 'Aaaah! Me Argentina, hahahaha!' Gripping an imaginary machine gun, she starts making machine-gun noises at us at a volume that threatens to drown out the screams of the by now very angry prostitute. We run back to the hotel.

Day two: we awaken to the buzz of a telephone that we didn't know we had. Reception informs us that our friend is waiting for us outside. We look out of the window and see our gangster friend sitting on the kerb. He looks annoyed. We leave him sitting there for three hours whilst we decide how best to survive another day in this horrible, horrible city before getting the hell out of there on a bus later that night. We eventually creep downstairs and bump straight into him. He tells us that he has the drugs we ordered from him the day before (which is a surprise considering that we hadn't), and that not going with him to collect them would result in injury. To get rid of him, we pay him half of the money and arrange to meet him for lunch. We jump straight into the nearest taxi and hide silently in the bus station for the rest of the day.

THEO BONHAM CARTER

CRAP VACATION TRIVIA

BEWARE OF THE GIRAFFE

A giraffe thought to be responsible for killing an American tourist in a game reserve in Kenya hurled itself off a cliff to evade capture in 2002. It is thought the tourist forgot that the giraffe was wild and got too close while walking in the Aberdale Country Club near Nairobi. James Drysdale, duty manager of the Country Club, commented, 'Once a giraffe takes it into its head to do something, that is it.'

04 CARAVANNING IN NORTH WALES

STRESS	💩 💩 💩 💩 ·
SICKNESS	💩 💩 💩 💩 ·
BOREDOM	💩 💩 💩 💩 💩
DANGER	💩 💩 💩 💩 ·
EXPLOITATION	💩 · · · ·

Duration: 2 weeks
Cost: $210

I have had so many tortuous childhood vacations to Wales (is there any other kind?) that most of them have merged into one vast, dull, dry pie, its ingredients being the old reliables of driving rain, freezing railway platforms, tedious castles, grotty food and family rows. However, there was one year in particular that stands out firmly like a javelin of indestructible misery in my mind. Not because of the ceaseless machine-gunning rain that greeted us every single sodding morning, the raindrops not only tapping relentlessly like a bionic clock constantly reminding you of

WALES WILL BLOW YOU AWAY

133

your life wasting away, but also sounding like the hammering of a million nails, securing you permanently to these yawn-infested surroundings. Neither was it because, even though our week in Wales was always utter shite, this particular year my dad—in a fit of sadism—decided to book us in for a fortnight. And no, no, no—it's not because I tripped over a fencepost and ripped my thigh apart on a rusty nail causing me and my weeping mother to spend six hours in Casualty while it was sewn up. (Actually, that was one of the merrier highlights, closely followed by my sister puking her coccyx up in the back of the car on day two, leaving the seats to fester and stink for the entire vacation.) No. The reason that this vacation was the fucking shittest experience of my entire childhood was because, instead of the usual annual moping listlessly about in some draughty joy-free rented cottage, this time we were stuck in a fucking caravan held together by rust in a field boasting a bumper harvest of bovine excrement. The caravan leaked, the mattresses were mouldy, the toilet was broken and to make matters worse my little sister and I were frequently booted out of the van so my parents could get amorous with each other. That left us nowhere to turn but the park's 'entertainment room'. Such a grand title for a cold bare room with a pool table that only had four balls and, tauntingly, a video recorder—hey, space age technology—but no TV. Skulking about there meant being prodded, punched and Chinese-burned by older, even more pissed-off kids whose only other activity involved smoking pinched fags.

Vacation brochures always include a few glorious sun-kissed beaches where you can imagine yourself building castles and tearing off with newfound friends into the warm sea for swimming races and hunting for shells or crabs. Our beach was a windswept bastard of crushed beer cans, smashed bottles and abandoned deck chairs rolling miserably in solitude. It was there I learnt why lemmings hurl themselves off cliffs. And I envied them.

DAN HAMILTON

03 WAIKIKI BEACH, HAWAII

STRESS	💩	💩	💩	💩	•
SICKNESS	💩	💩	💩	•	•
BOREDOM	💩	💩	•	•	•
DANGER	💩	💩	💩	•	•
EXPLOITATION	💩	💩	💩	•	•

Duration: 1 week
Cost: $1200

The glossy vacation brochures were lying. Forget swaying palms trees and the gentle Pacific sea breeze. Imagine instead a tangle of towering, grimy multi-storey hotels and the constant torrent of traffic, chugging out fumes and loud rap music.

If you stagger down the dingy boulevards, searching in vain for paradise, you'll be confronted instead by crowds of saggy, middle-aged Americans squeezed into sweaty shorts and flowery muumuus, while sullen young men in baggy Quiksilver pants swing their grubby surfboards into your path. The oily aroma of cheeseburger and large fries only just masks the stench of the nearby Alai Wai canal.

Waikiki Beach, so glamorous on the television, is a disappointingly thin curve of sand piled high with motionless burned bodies. But this is not hell, this is a sunbathers' heaven. It said so in the brochure. If you prefer your torture Hawaiian-style, you can allow yourself to be sneered at for an hour by a surf instructor, who will drag you out into the waves and laugh heartily as you flip off your board and dash your knees against the spiky reef. At least in the evening you can sit back and enjoy a beer. As long as you have three forms of ID and can convince the waitress you are not a sixteen-year-old punk who will get her fired for serving an underage drinker. Fail this test and you will face a long, miserable night in your dingy hotel room. Maybe locking yourself in your room is the best option. At least then you can sip a warm Bud in peace and tend to your surfing wounds. Waikiki looked nice on *Magnum, P.I.*, didn't it?

CLAIRE BRADSHAW

CRAP VACATION TRIVIA

Per capita, more Spam gets eaten on Hawaii than any other place on earth.

'A TANGLE OF TOWERING GRIMY MULTI-STOREY HOTELS'

02 SCARBOROUGH, ENGLAND

STRESS	💩 💩 💩 · ·
SICKNESS	💩 💩 💩 💩 💩
BOREDOM	💩 💩 💩 💩 💩
DANGER	💩 💩 💩 · ·
EXPLOITATION	· · · · ·

Duration: 2 weeks
Cost: $850

From the age of one until I was fifteen every single fucking vacation I had was spent at my grandparents' in Scarborough.

My dad didn't like going away. He liked his position on the sofa; he liked his seat in the local pub and most of all, his garage full of bikes and tools. For him the very idea of a 'vacation' was anathema.

Six hours there, the same service stations, the same views, the same horrors of industry smoking on the horizon until finally we would arrive at the same bungalow in Scalby.

In the course of the next week we would travel up and down the coast from base camp, having vast landscapes pointed out to us, eating warm sand-wiches and moaning, perpetually. Not just Dad but us kids, bored shitless in the back of a Maxi, then an Avenger, then a Volvo, the latter being the family workhorse for a good decade. Mum, as always, was the voice of reason, calm and gentle until she too succumbed to the growing voices of dissent before going fucking crazy. Then we'd all go quiet again. Dad would gradually become 'The Appeaser'. If any of us so much as sniffed he'd chide us, his eyes darting between the road, us kids and Mum as he sought her approval for his parenting skills in order to win back her favour. Once gained he always lost it again, usu-ally in the form of Krakatoa farts, not to mention the occasional belch resulting in disappointed moans from Mum and laughing from the cheap seats. Nothing made my dad's day more than a well-timed passing of wind, the louder and more odorous the better as far as he was concerned, even if it resulted in a fully blown shit-stained disaster.

After miles and miles of road our legs became welded to the vinyl seats and

our tiny frames became one with the car, the view of the backs of my parents heads rocking on their headrests became burned into our minds. By the end of the vacation, it was all we could remember, apart from the last day before we went home when we were always let loose on all the amusements (or 'amazements' according to my sister) on Scarborough's South and North Bays.

Apart from the car, possibly the most awful place was the beach, in particular Boggle Hole near Robin Hood's Bay, which had more than a whiff of *Straw Dogs* about it. The late, great Bill Hicks couldn't understand the beach, 'it's where dirt meets water', he proclaimed and I agree, especially ones facing the North Sea. We would sit there like penguins huddling from the violent blasts of sand, and freezing wind. It was sheer torture.

When there was a gap in God's sand-blasting schedule we would venture tentatively towards rock pools and use sticks to poke at the habitat, stabbing at anything that moved or dropping larger rocks on whatever poor bastard creature had dared to exist peacefully in its environment. Worse still was the actual sea; sludge grey and so ludicrously cold that it was impossible to work out why it was still liquid. But for some reason paddling was the one activity my dad didn't mind (presumably he thought of it as some kind of penitence), and if Dad paddled we all paddled by default. The subsequent sand removal operation from Dad's feet wasn't dissimilar to water torture. By the time it came to servicing said feet, the sea was half a mile away and had exposed another beach of razor-sharp shale and the occasional dead jellyfish. We all plodded miles out with little fucking buckets, braved the now nitrogen cold water and plodded back with rapidly diminishing stocks of seawater (the wind would literally blow it out) for the sole purpose of pouring it over Dad's feet.

Still it wasn't all bad, the best incident by far was when my younger brother shat himself whilst standing on a breakwater; such was the weight of this behemoth stool it pulled the back of his trunks down. I thought my dad was going to die, as he was totally incapacitated through laughing. I can still see my mum being blown about on the beach in the far distance, swinging what looked like a small striped bag and flinging its contents into the freezing North Sea. My shivering, towel-clad and considerably lighter brother in the arms of my sister while Dad gurgled like the village idiot. The trunks came home with us in a plastic Sainsbury's bag. Of course the altogether familiar insides of the car now stank to high heaven all the way back to Granny and Granddad's—for the umpteenth fucking time.

JAMIE DWELLY

THE FIVE MOST IMMORAL VACATIONS ON EARTH

5 THE 'PRIVATIZED' KILLING FIELDS OF CAMBODIA

Three million people, a quarter of Cambodia's entire population, died through starvation, illness, execution and torture under Pol Pot's Khmer Rouge regime. In April 2005 the mayor of Phnom Penh, Kep Chuktema, signed a thirty-year contract with JC Royal, a private Japanese company, to manage 'The Killing Fields'–the nation's mass grave memorial. Under the terms of the deal JC Royal will increase tourist entrance fees by 500% while reportedly paying the government an annual leasing fee of just $15,500. Local people, who were previously allowed in without charge, will now have to cough up an entrance fee whenever they want to pay their respects to lost relatives. Despite protests from many locals who believe the spirits of the victims are being traded for money, the mayor believed the move was justified. 'We need to beautify the site to attract tourists,' he said, in response to their concerns.

❹ THE 2008 OLYMPICS, BEIJING

A Chinese dissident suggested that before the IOC granted Beijing the privilege of hosting the Olympics, the government should be forced to release all of its political prisoners. The members of the IOC skulked around with the collective expression of someone pretending not to have noticed a fart in the room while the Chinese government had her arrested and sentenced to two years' 're-education through labour'.

Still, even though China has such a horrifying reputation when it comes to human rights, visitors will be pleased to hear that thanks to the impending Olympic arrival there's less pollution in Beijing now and they've planted lots more trees.

3 TREKKING IN NEPAL, PERU AND TANZANIA

Trekkers have a reputation for being responsible and forward thinking—seeking greater challenges from their time off than the traditional holidaymaker. But porters working the popular trekking routes of the Inca trail, the Himalayas and Kilimanjaro are systematically used as pack horses to carry luggage in a practice more at home in the days of the Empire than today. Despite the risks of frostbite, exhaustion, exposure and hypothermia, few porters can afford appropriate clothing, which leads to frostbite for many as they trudge through the snow wearing sandals. Porters have died from exhaustion while carrying tourists' belongings, and recently there have been reports of them being abandoned in life-threatening blizzards while trekkers are air lifted to safety in helicopters. In the words of a Peruvian porters' syndicate, 'We suffer humiliation upon humiliation, and are treated as less than human.'

2 THE MALDIVES

The Maldives, with their deserted white sandy beaches, palm trees and crystal-clear seas, epitomize, for many of us, paradise on earth. At around $3500 per person for an all-inclusive two-week vacation, it is one of the most popular luxury vacation destinations on the planet.

Life for local people is a rather different experience from that of its guests. The Maldives is not a member of the International Labor Organization, there is no minimum wage for the private sector, there is no statutory provision for hours of work, there are no laws governing health and safety conditions and there are no trade unions. Over half the 20,000 people employed in tourism in the Maldives come from Sri Lanka, India, Pakistan and Bangladesh (many of whom pay an agent in their own country up to $700 for each job). To earn the average wage of $75 per month tourist workers toil for twelve hours a day, seven days a week and only have one day off a month.

Workers' living conditions on the tourist islands are cramped, with up to fifteen of them sharing a single room. One worker told Tourism Concern, 'When you live and work in a resort, there is no social life. All your time is spent working, and I only see my family once a year.'

WHILE TOURISTS ENJOY DESERTED BEACHES, LOCALS ENDURE SEVERE OVERCROWDING. IN MALE, ONE OF THE NON-TOURIST MALDIVIAN ISLANDS, THERE IS A POPULATION DENSITY OF 40,000 PER SQ KM (ONE OF THE HIGHEST RATES IN THE WORLD)

1 BURMA

'...Quiet lakes, temples and pagodas, pristine beaches...A step back in time...still undeveloped and a wonderful experience.'–Burmese tourist brochure.

A military junta controlled by General Ne Win has governed Burma for the last forty years. The head of the Burmese opposition party, Nobel prize-winner Aung San Suu Kyi, won a landslide victory in Burma's national elections in 1990. Despite this, she has spent a total of eight years between 1989 and 2002 under house arrest. She was detained again in May 2003 and in December 2004 General Ne Win announced that she would remain incarcerated for at least another year.

In an attempt to rebrand the country as a tourist destination in 1996 the junta renamed Burma 'Myanmar' and declared it 'Visit Myanmar Year' at tourist conferences across the globe. But this new vacation paradise has been constructed at a terrible human cost. According to the UN International Labor Organization eight milllion men women and children are conscripted into forced labour camps every year. 'The military...treat the civilian population as an unlimited pool of unpaid forced labourers and servants at their disposal. The practice of

forced labour is to encourage private investment in infrastructure development, public sector works and tourism projects.' Reports have emerged of systematic abuse, including the rape and torture of thousands of Burmese people and the displacement of countless others as the junta exploit the free labour of their populace to construct much of the infrastructure required of any modern tourist destination. UK foreign office minister Mike O'Brien urged holidaymakers to think twice before travelling to Burma. 'Foreign visitors remain a source of hard currency for the regime, much of which ends up in the private bank accounts of the generals and their associates.' Despite repeated requests from Aung San Suu Kyi, and campaigners, Lonely Planet still publishes a guide to Burma. Campaigners are calling for a boycott of all Lonely Planet Guides in protest.

Tourism Concern is running campaigns against tourism in Burma, the abuse of porters in Nepal, Peru and Tanzania and the exploitation of workers in the Maldives.
To view all their campaigns visit
http://www.tourismconcern.org.uk/

01 SUNNY BEACH, BULGARIA

STRESS	💩 💩 💩 💩 ·
SICKNESS	💩 💩 💩 💩 ·
BOREDOM	💩 💩 💩 💩 ·
DANGER	💩 💩 💩 💩 💩
EXPLOITATION	💩 💩 💩 · ·

Duration: 2 weeks
Cost: $4400

I realized something wasn't quite right about this family vacation to Bulgaria on the Balkan Airlines plane on the way out. The in-flight meal was a cucumber salad, which involved cutting whole cucumbers in half and presenting each passenger with half a cucumber—not sliced or peeled or washed—just half a cucumber and nothing else.

The wreaths of cigarette smoke from the many smokers a few inches away on the opposite aisle forced me to complain because we had specifically asked to sit in the non-smoking area. 'You are,' said the stewardess. 'The whole of the left side is non-smoking and the right side is smoking.'

The hotel on 'Sunny Beach' seemed to be mainly occupied by seriously drunk Swedish guys taking advantage of the beer at ten pence a pint; some of them appeared to have messed their pants at some time over their stay. One particular guy was scarily loud and aggressive, and although the hotel had hundreds of rooms it was of course inevitable that he occupied the one above ours. His favourite sport was to scour the hotel for glass ashtrays to smash down on to our balcony into the small hours. In our room it appeared at first as though the previous occupants had wet the bed but fortunately it turned out just to be damp accumulated over the winter as the sheets waited for us to arrive. The family vacation consisted of my Yorkshire in-laws, their six children and partners with a few grandchildren chucked in for good measure. We all headed off for the poshest restaurant we could find where the choice was Veal, Vienna Schnitzel or Chef's Surprise, which was veal but it did come with a choice of three salads—tomato, cucumber or mixed salad. We went for mixed, which was of course the first two mixed together. The following night we tried the next poshest restaurant as it boasted chicken. The seventeen of us were first in when it opened. 'What would you like?' said the waiter. 'Chicken please,' said the first. 'OK,' said the waiter, 'and the next?' 'Chicken for me too.' 'Sorry, sold out,' he said. We asked for a bottle of their best Bulgarian wine. 'That will be from Morocco then,' he said. 'We relabel it and export it to England.' And so it went on. From the beach strewn with broken ashtray glass and the thousands of sellers on the beach (NO. I DON'T WANT TO BUY ANY FUCKING SHELLS!), to the indoor hotel pools mysteriously full with water and soil. 'When do you sleep?' I asked the hotel manager (cum-night-porter-cum-waiter-cum-illegal moneychanger) as we left. 'September,' he grinned, 'till then the drugs.' **JOHN JOHNSTONE**

INDEX

About the Editor

DAN KIERAN is deputy editor of *Idler* magazine.
He lives in London with his girlfriend, Rachel,
and their son, Wilf.

MORE CRAP FROM DAN KIERAN

CRAP JOBS
100 Tales of Workplace Hell

ISBN 0-06-083341-6 (paperback)

From the geniuses behind *The Idler*, comes this hysterical compendium of the most humiliating, soul-destroying, immoral, and crappiest jobs out there, as evidenced by the brave souls who perform them daily. If you thought your job was bad, try comparing it to a maggot farmer or phone sex operator, two jobs ranked by Kieran as both "humiliating" and "disgusting." However, Kieran doesn't confine himself to the weird, he also includes jobs such as bank teller ("soul-destroying"), broadcast executive ("humiliating," "futile," "soul-destroying," and "immoral"), and editorial assistant ("humiliating" and "soul-destroying"). *Crap Jobs* brings firsthand accounts from the people doing the absolute worst and most degrading jobs.